VOLUME 4

URSULA LE GUIN TO HELEN OXENBURY

FAVORITE CHILDREN'S
AUTHORS AND
ILLUSTRATORS

E. RUSSELL PRIMM III, EDITOR IN CHIEF

TRADITION BOOKS™
EXCELSIOR, MINNESOTA

*For Irene Barron Keller, whose love of the English language touched
the lives of millions of young readers through her writing and editing*

∾

Published by **TRADITION BOOKS**™ and distributed to
the school and library market by **THE CHILD'S WORLD**®
P.O. Box 326, Chanhassen, MN 55317-0326
800/599-READ
http://www.childsworld.com

A NOTE TO OUR READERS:

The publication dates listed in each author or illustrator's selected bibliography represent the date
of first publication in the United States.

The editors have listed literary awards that were announced prior to August 2002.

Every effort has been made to contact copyright holders of material included in this reference work.
If any errors or omissions have occurred, corrections will be made in future editions.

Photographs ©: Candlewick Press: 152; de Grummond Children's Literature Collection, University
of Southern Mississippi: 16, 48, 72; Farrar, Straus and Giroux: 12; Harcourt: 8 (Marion Wood
Kolisch), 52, 132; HarperCollins Publishers: 24, 64 (Judy B. Messer), 108 (Bachrach), 120
(Constance Myers), 136 (Barry E. Levine); Henry Holt and Company: 80; Houghton Mifflin
Company: 144; Karen Mohn: 44; Katherine Lambert Photography: 124; Kerlan Collection,
University of Minnesota: 28 (Gillman and Soame), 32 (Riwkin Stockholm/Sweden), 88 (Viking
Press), 128 (C. Cady); Library of Congress: 112; Scholastic: 20 (Milan Sabatini), 76, 92, 100, 104,
116, 148; Simon & Schuster: 40 (Marilyn Sanders), 96 (Misha), 140.

An Editorial Directions book

LIBRARY OF CONGRESS CATALOGING-IN-PUBLICATION DATA

Favorite children's authors and illustrators / E. Russell Primm, III, editor-in-chief.
    p. cm.
Summary: Provides biographical information about authors and illustrators of books for children
and young adults, arranged in dictionary form. Includes bibliographical references and index.
  ISBN 1-59187-018-6 (v. 1 : lib. bdg. : alk. paper)—ISBN 1-59187-019-4 (v. 2 : lib. bdg. : alk.
paper)—ISBN 1-59187-020-8 (v. 3 : lib. bdg. : alk. paper)—ISBN 1-59187-021-6 (v. 4 : lib. bdg. :
alk. paper)—ISBN 1-59187-022-4 (v. 5 : lib. bdg. : alk. paper)—ISBN 1-59187-023-2 (v. 6 : lib.
bdg. : alk. paper) 1. Children's literature—Bio-bibliography—Dictionaries—Juvenile literature.
2. Illustrators—Biography—Dictionaries—Juvenile literature. [1. Authors. 2. Illustrators.]
I. Primm, E. Russell, 1958–
 PN1009.A1 F38 2002
  809'.89282'03—dc21   2002007129

TABLE OF CONTENTS

Major Children's Author and Illustrator Literary Awards

The American Book Award
Awarded from 1980 to 1983 in place of the National Book Award to give national recognition to achievement in several categories of children's literature. Established in 1978 to recognize outstanding literary achievement by contemporary American authors

The Boston Globe-Horn Book Awards
Established in 1967 by Horn Book *magazine and the* Boston Globe *newspaper to honor the year's best fiction, poetry, nonfiction, and picture books for children*

The Caldecott Medal
Established in 1938 and presented by the Association for Library Service to Children division of the American Library Association to illustrators for the most distinguished picture book for children from the preceding year

The Carnegie Medal
Established in 1936 and presented by the British Library Association for an outstanding book for children written in English

The Carter G. Woodson Book Award
Established in 1974 and presented by the National Council for the Social Studies for the most distinguished social science books appropriate for young readers that depict ethnicity in the United States

The Coretta Scott King Awards
Established in 1970 in connection with the American Library Association to honor African-American authors and illustrators whose books are deemed outstanding, educational, and inspirational

The Hans Christian Andersen Medal
Established in 1956 by the International Board on Books for Young People to honor an author or illustrator, living at the time of nomination, whose complete works have made a lasting contribution to children's literature

THE KATE GREENAWAY MEDAL

Established by the Youth Libraries Group of the British Library Association in 1956 to honor illustrators of children's books published in the United Kingdom

THE LAURA INGALLS WILDER AWARD

Established by the Association for Library Service to Children division of the American Library Association in 1954 to honor an author or illustrator whose books, published in the United States, have made a substantial and lasting contribution to children's literature

THE MICHAEL L. PRINTZ AWARD

Established by the Young Adult Library Services division of the American Library Association in 2000 to honor literary excellence in young adult literature (fiction, nonfiction, poetry, or anthology)

THE NATIONAL BOOK AWARD

Established in 1950 to give national recognition to achievement in fiction, nonfiction, poetry, and young people's literature

THE NEWBERY MEDAL

Established in 1922 and presented by the Association for Library Service to Children division of the American Library Association for the most distinguished contribution to children's literature in the preceding year

THE ORBIS PICTUS AWARD FOR OUTSTANDING NONFICTION

Established in 1990 by the National Council of Teachers of English to honor an outstanding informational book published in the preceding year

THE PURA BELPRÉ AWARDS

Established in 1996 and cosponsored by the Association for Library Service to Children division of the American Library Association and the National Association to Promote Library Services to the Spanish Speaking to recognize a writer and illustrator of Latino or Latina background whose works affirm and celebrate the Latino experience

THE SCOTT O'DELL AWARD

Established in 1982 and presented by the O'Dell Award Committee to an American author who writes an outstanding tale of historical fiction for children or young adults that takes place in the New World

Ursula K. Le Guin

Born: October 21, 1929

Throughout her long career, Ursula K. Le Guin has consistently enjoyed shattering stereotypes. It was believed that only men could write science fiction. She quickly became one of the most popular and well respected science-fiction writers of all time. It was also believed that science-fiction writers couldn't write "serious" novels. Again, Le Guin established herself as a true literary novelist.

Ursula Le Guin was born on October 21, 1929 in Berkeley, California. Her father was an anthropologist who founded the anthropology department at the University of California at Berkeley. Her mother, Theodora Kroeber, was an author best known for her children's books, including *The Inland Whale* and *Ishi in Two Worlds: A Biography of the Last Wild Indian in North America*.

LE GUIN BELIEVES THAT ANY AUTHOR WHO WANTS TO WRITE FANTASY SHOULD USE J. R. R. TOLKIEN'S LORD OF THE RINGS SERIES AS A MODEL.

Growing up with such talented and intellectual parents, Ursula was constantly surrounded by books, and her young mind was always stimulated. Her curiosity and imagination grew rapidly. She recalls sitting around listening to grown-ups talk about "really interesting stuff." She soon began writing her own stories.

The first story Ursula submitted for publication was a science-fiction tale about time travel. She sent it to a popular science-fiction magazine. The story was rejected. Ursula was just eleven years old at the time. She was not discouraged and continued to write.

In 1947, Ursula Le Guin left California to attend Radcliffe College in Cambridge, Massachusetts. She then went to Columbia University in New York City for her master's degree. In 1953, she was aboard the ocean liner the *Queen Mary* on her way to study in France when she met Charles Le Guin. They married a few months later in Paris.

Returning to the United States, the Le Guins lived first in Macon, Georgia, and then settled in Portland, Oregon, where they still reside. Le Guin never stopped writing, turning out stories and poetry.

After seven years of rejection letters, she had the same story accepted by both a

> *"It's my job to listen for ideas, and welcome them when they come, and do something with them. I'm not saying it's easy. But there's nothing I'd rather do."*

A VERY VERSATILE WRITER, URSULA K. LE GUIN HAS WRITTEN
NOVELS, NOVELLAS, SHORT STORIES, POETRY, ESSAYS, TRANSLATIONS
OF OTHER WRITER'S WORKS, AND CHILDREN'S BOOKS.

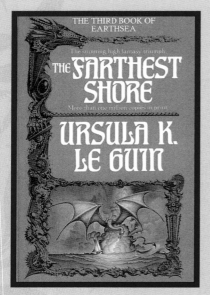

THE THIRD BOOK OF
EARTHSEA

The stunning, high fantasy triumph

THE FARTHEST
SHORE

More than one million copies in print

URSULA K.
LE GUIN

A Selected Bibliography of Le Guin's Work

Jane on Her Own: A Catwings Tale (1999)
Wonderful Alexander and the Catwings (1994)
A Ride on the Red Mare's Back (1992)
Catwings Return (1989)
Catwings (1988)
The Farthest Shore (1972)
The Tombs of Atuan (1971)
A Wizard of Earthsea (1968)
Rocannon's World (1966)

Le Guin's Major Literary Awards

1972 National Book Award
   The Farthest Shore
1972 Newbery Honor Book
   The Tombs of Atuan
1969 *Boston Globe–Horn Book* Fiction Award
   A Wizard of Earthsea

literary magazine and *Amazing Stories,* a science-fiction magazine. The tale, called "April in Paris," tells the story of figures from different historical periods who travel to fifteenth-century Paris to meet and marry. The literary magazine offered no money; *Amazing Stories* offered her thirty dollars for her story. She chose the science-fiction publication.

"Thirty dollars meant a lot to us back then," she explains. And so she began reading a lot of science fiction and working on improving her writing in the genre. Ursula K. Le Guin's first novel was *Rocannon's World,* published in 1966. Other novels, novellas, and short stories followed. In 1968, she published the first book in her Earthsea trilogy, *A Wizard of Earthsea. The Tombs of Atuan* and *The Farthest Shore* followed, completing one of the most beloved fantasy trilogies of all time. Like much of her work, this trilogy features strong female characters, breaking yet another stereotype in the science-fiction and fantasy genres.

Ursula K. Le Guin is proud of the fact she has brought science fiction to many new readers. "I do seem to be someone who has carried people across from realistic literature to fantasy and science fiction, and back," she explains. "I'm happy to do that. If I'm a stepping stone, walk on me, for heaven's sake." It's a walk her loyal readers are thrilled to take.

❧

WHERE TO FIND OUT MORE ABOUT URSULA K. LE GUIN

BOOKS

Reid, Suzanne Elizabeth. *Presenting Ursula Le Guin.* New York: Twayne Publishers, 1997.

Sutherland, Zena. *Children and Books.* New York: Addison Wesley Longman, 1997.

WEB SITES

LE GUIN'S WORLD
http://hem.passagen.se/peson42/lgw/bio.html
For a biographical sketch of Ursula K. Le Guin and a link to a booklist

URSULA K. LE GUIN'S WEB PAGE
http://www.ursulakleguin.com/Bio2001.html
To read a biographical sketch of Ursula K. Le Guin

ALTHOUGH MANY OF HER STORIES TAKE PLACE IN THE FUTURE IN FARAWAY ALIEN WORLDS, URSULA K. LE GUIN ADDRESSES MANY OF THE SAME SUBJECTS AS REALISTIC FICTION, SUCH AS HUMAN NATURE, POLITICS, AND FEELINGS.

Madeleine L'Engle

Born: November 29, 1918

Madeleine L'Engle does not have many happy memories of her school days. She attended a boarding school in Switzerland, where she felt that she did not fit in. Instead of paying attention in school, she thought about a poem or a story she was writing. Her interest in writing continued throughout her life. L'Engle has published plays, poems, and novels for both children and adults. Her most popular books for children include the Time Fantasy series and the Austin Family series.

Madeleine L'Engle was born on November 29, 1918, in New York City. Her mother was a pianist and her father was a journalist. Her parents had many friends who were artists, writers, and

L'ENGLE'S REAL NAME IS MADELEINE FRANKLIN, BUT SHE ALWAYS USES THE NAME L'ENGLE FOR HER WRITING.

musicians. Madeleine was surrounded by creative people who encouraged her to use her imagination. She was always writing stories and poems. She wrote her first stories when she was five years old.

When she was twelve years old, Madeleine and her family moved to Europe. They lived in France and Switzerland. Madeleine was a shy girl and felt like an outsider at her Swiss boarding school. Writing was much more important to Madeleine than school was.

Madeleine and her family returned to the United States so she could attend high school. She enjoyed school much more as a student in Charleston, South Carolina.

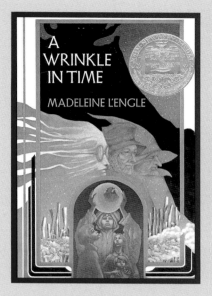

A Selected Bibliography of L'Engle's Work

The Other Dog (2001)
Full House: An Austin Family Christmas (1999)
Miracle on 10th Street & Other Christmas Writings (1998)
Troubling a Star (1994)
The Glorious Impossible (1990)
Many Waters (1986)
A Ring of Endless Light (1980)
A Swiftly Tilting Planet (1978)
A Wind in the Door (1973)
The Young Unicorns (1968)
The Arm of the Starfish (1965)
The Moon by Night (1963)
A Wrinkle in Time (1962)
Meet the Austins (1960)

L'Engle's Major Literary Awards

1981 Newbery Honor Book
   A Ring of Endless Light

1980 American Book Award
   A Swiftly Tilting Planet

1963 Newbery Medal
   A Wrinkle in Time

> "The world is changing rapidly—that terrifies people. We know a great deal more now about the nature of the universe than we used to, which I think makes it all the more exciting. But change is frightening to people. And when you get frightened, you strike out."

After graduating from high school, Madeleine L'Engle attended Smith College. She studied English and continued to work on her creative writing. She graduated in 1941 and moved to New York City.

In New York, L'Engle worked as an actress in theater productions. She also had time to write. She published her first two novels while living in New York. She also met an actor named Hugh Franklin and married him in 1946. The couple later had three children.

L'Engle and her family moved to Connecticut. She and her husband owned a general store. Operating the store and raising her children kept L'Engle busy. She did not have much time to write. She could concentrate on her writing at only night when the house was quiet. The family eventually moved back to New York City. Her husband continued his acting career. L'Engle began to find great success as a writer.

L'Engle's most popular children's book is *A Wrinkle in Time*. The book was rejected by twenty-six publishers before it was published in 1962. Many publishers thought the book was too difficult for young

---

L'ENGLE HAS BEEN THE LIBRARIAN AT THE CATHEDRAL CHURCH OF ST. JOHN THE DIVINE IN NEW YORK CITY FOR MORE THAN THIRTY YEARS.

readers. It turned out to be very popular and led to four other books in the Time Fantasy series.

L'Engle has won many awards for her books. She lives in New York City and continues to write books for both young people and adults.

> *"I had to write. I had no choice in the matter. It was not up to me to say I would stop, because I could not. It didn't matter how small or inadequate my talent. If I never had another book published . . . I still had to go on writing."*

Where to Find Out More About Madeleine L'Engle

Books

Gonzales, Doreen. *Madeleine L'Engle: Author of* A Wrinkle in Time. New York: Macmillan, 1991.

Kovacs, Deborah, and James Preller. *Meet the Authors and Illustrators: 60 Creators of Favorite Children's Books Talk about Their Work*. Vol. 1. New York: Scholastic, 1991.

Web Sites

Amazon.com: A Conversation with Madeleine L'Engle
http://www.amazon.com/exec/obidos/ts/feature/6238/002-6906564-3054408
To read an interview with Madeleine L'Engle

Educational Paperback Association
http://www.edupaperback.org/authorbios/LEngle_Madeleine.html
To read an autobiographical sketch of and a booklist for Madeleine L'Engle

A movie-production company purchased the rights to the first three books in L'Engle's Time Fantasy series. The movie version of *A Wrinkle in Time* is in production.

Lois Lenski

Born: October 14, 1893
Died: September 11, 1974

Growing up in a small town was an important part of Lois Lenski's life. Her experiences and memories of growing up can be seen in her books. Lenski illustrated more than fifty books for other authors. She wrote and illustrated more than 100 of her own books. She also wrote poetry, plays, and songs for children herself. Her books for children and young people include *Cowboy Small, Grandmother Tippytoe, Strawberry Girl,* and *Indian Captive: The Story of Mary Jemison.*

Lois Lenski was born on October 14, 1893, in Springfield, Ohio. Her father was the pastor of a church. When she was six years old, Lois and her family moved to Anna,

LENSKI BELIEVED THAT CHILDREN'S BOOKS SHOULD DO MORE THAN ENTERTAIN. SHE WANTED THEM TO "ILLUMINE THE WHOLE ADVENTURE OF LIVING."

Ohio, a small rural town. Lois loved her life in this community. "It offered all a child could enjoy and comprehend," she later noted. "Commonplace and ordinary, it had no particular beauty or grace, but it soon became my own."

Learning was important in Lois's family. Her parents encouraged her to read and to work hard in school. They wanted their children to be able to go to college. Lois read many books and also liked to draw. She would spend hours copying pictures from books and magazines.

The town of Anna was so small it did not have a high school. Lois had to take a train each day to a nearby town to attend high school. She graduated in 1911, and her family then moved to Columbus, Ohio. Lois Lenski enrolled as a student at Ohio State University, where she studied to be a teacher. She also took classes in drawing and art. When Lenski graduated, her parents thought she would become a teacher. She instead took the advice of one of her art professors. She moved to New York City to study at the Art Students League.

> *"I have a strong urge to work, I am not happy unless I am at work. I believe this compulsion to work was not only a part of my conscious training, but also a part of my Polish inheritance."*

THE DAVY SERIES WAS BASED ON LENSKI'S GRANDSON, DAVID, WHO LIVED WITH HER DURING THREE SUMMER VACATIONS.

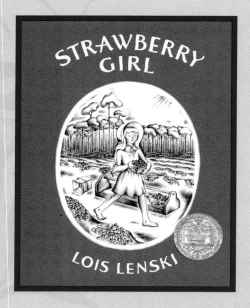

A Selected Bibliography of Lenski's Work

Chimney Corner Stories: Tales for Little Children (Illustrations only, 1992)

Sing a Song of People (1987)

Debbie and Her Pets (1971)

Debbie Goes to Nursery School (1970)

High-Rise Secret (1966)

Davy Goes Places (1961)

Cowboy Small (1949)

Judy's Journey (1947)

Strawberry Girl (1945)

Bayou Suzette (1943)

Indian Captive: The Story of Mary Jemison (1941)

Phebe Fairchild, Her Book (1936)

Grandmother Tippytoe (1931)

Skipping Village (1927)

City Poems (1971)

Lenski's Major Literary Awards

1946 Newbery Medal
   Strawberry Girl

1942 Newbery Honor Book
   Indian Captive: The Story of Mary Jemison

1937 Newbery Honor Book
   Phoebe Fairchild, Her Book

She studied for four years and took part-time jobs to support herself. She worked on lettering greeting cards and drawing fashion advertisements. She met an artist named Arthur Covey and helped him paint his murals. After a trip to Europe to study art, she returned to New York and married Covey.

In 1918, Lenski was hired to illustrate the *Children's Frieze Book*. She went on to illustrate more books for other authors

"My poems are the very essence, the fabric behind all my work for children. The themes in them are my life's blood. They are my legacy to the children I love."

including the Betsy Tacy series by Maud Hart Lovelace. Lenski published her first book, *Skipping Village,* in 1927. Many of Lenski's books have a historical focus. She often used fictional characters in her books to tell real stories.

Lenski continued writing throughout the 1950s and 1960s. Her last book was published in 1972. Lenski died at her home in Florida on September 11, 1974.

❧

WHERE TO FIND OUT MORE ABOUT LOIS LENSKI

BOOKS

Lenski, Lois. *Journey into Childhood: The Autobiography of Lois Lenski.*
Philadelphia: Lippincott, 1972.

Sutherland, Zena. *Children and Books.*
New York: Longman, 1997.

WEB SITES

MILNER LIBRARY: ILLINOIS STATE UNIVERSITY
http://www.mlb.ilstu.edu/ressubj/speccol/lenski/Welcome.html
To read a biographical sketch of and a booklist for Lois Lenski

PURPLE HOUSE PRESS
http://www.purplehousepress.com/sig/lenskibio.htm
To read a biographical sketch of Lois Lenski

THE BOOK *COWBOY SMALL* WAS ADAPTED INTO
A MOTION-PICTURE SCREENPLAY IN **1955.**

> "*I am not sure what led me to become a writer. There was no decision. Rather there was a growing certainty that grew from the age of seventeen until I was twenty-one that this was what I was supposed to do with my life.*"

legendary blues and folk musician Leadbelly. It was also Lester's first published work.

As Lester got more involved with the civil rights movement, he applied his love of photography to recording key events in the movement. His photos are now part of the Smithsonian Institution and document this important period in U.S. history. Lester also wrote many books for adults about black history, politics, and civil rights.

During this time, Lester produced and hosted a radio program on WBAI-FM, a noncommercial radio station in New York City, that served as the voice of many emerging political movements in the 1960s. He also produced a program on WNET, New York public radio.

Lester's publisher urged him to write children's books. His first book for young readers was *To Be a Slave.* It asked readers to imagine what it was like to be a slave. Three of Lester's great-grandparents had been slaves, and the need to learn more about his personal past led him to study the subject. His next book for children, *Black Folktales,* also explored African-American history, folklore, and politics.

Lester continues to write books for both adults and children based on

IN ADDITION TO RECORDING TWO ALBUMS OF ORIGINAL SONGS, LESTER PERFORMED WITH FOLK MUSIC GREATS PETE SEEGER, PHIL OCHS, AND JUDY COLLINS.

his own family history and the history of African-Americans. "Sometimes I feel like there are all these spirits of blacks inside me, people who never had the opportunity to tell their stories, and they have chosen me to be their voice." His readers are fortunate to have the chance to listen to those voices.

> *"I write because the lives of all of us are stories. If enough of those stories are told, then perhaps we will begin to see that our lives are the same story. The differences are merely in the details."*

WHERE TO FIND OUT MORE ABOUT JULIUS LESTER

BOOKS

Fogelsong, Marilee. *Lives and Works: Young Adult Authors.* Danbury, Conn.: Grolier, 1999.

Hill, Christine M. *Ten Terrific Authors for Teens.* Berkeley Heights, N.J.: Enslow, 2000.

Rockman, Connie C., ed. *Eighth Book of Junior Authors and Illustrators.* New York: H. W. Wilson Company, 2000.

WEB SITES

AMAZON.COM: INTERVIEW WITH JULIUS LESTER
http://www.amazon.com/exec/obidos/show-interview/l-j-esterulius/002-6906564-3054408
To read an interview with Julius Lester

SCHOLASTIC ONLINE BIOGRAPHY
http://www2.scholastic.com/teachers/authorsandbooks/authorstudies/authorhome.jhtml?authorID=53&collateralID=5214&displayName=Biography
To read an autobiographical sketch of Julius Lester and a booklist

---

LESTER WRITES TWO TO THREE HOURS A DAY WHEN HE IS BEGINNING A BOOK, AND ALMOST NONSTOP WHEN HE NEARS THE END. HIS MAJOR DISTRACTION IS PLAYING CARD GAMES ON THE COMPUTER.

C. S. Lewis

Born: November 29, 1898
Died: November 22, 1963

C. S. Lewis was a literary critic, religious writer, poet, and science-fiction novelist. Most of his writing was for an adult audience. But Lewis is also remembered as a children's author. He wrote the Chronicles of Narnia series. The series begins with *The Lion, the Witch and the Wardrobe* and includes six additional titles.

Clive Staples (C. S.) Lewis was born on November 29, 1898, in Belfast, Ireland. "Jack," as he was nicknamed, was surrounded by books as a young child. He was a good student and did well in school. He spent most of his time reading books and writing stories. When Jack was ten years old, his mother became sick and died.

Jack and his brother were not close to their father. After their mother's death, they

---

LEWIS DIED ON THE SAME DAY THAT
PRESIDENT JOHN F. KENNEDY WAS ASSASSINATED.

were sent to boarding school, where Jack did not have pleasant experiences. He had a hard time concentrating on his studies. After a while, Jack's father hired a teacher to tutor him. The tutor helped Jack focus on his studies and prepared him for college.

Lewis first attended Oxford University in 1916. After less than a year at Oxford, he joined the British army and was sent to France. He was wounded during fighting in World War I (1914–1918). He returned to England to recover from his injuries. Once he was healthy, he continued his studies.

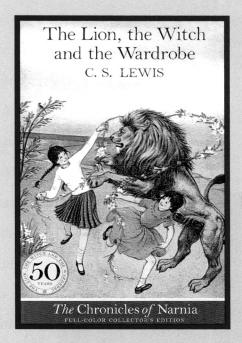

A Selected Bibliography of Lewis's Work

The Last Battle (1956)
The Magician's Nephew (1955)
The Horse and His Boy (1954)
The Silver Chair (1953)
The Voyage of the Dawn Treader (1952)
Prince Caspian (1951)
The Lion, the Witch and the Wardrobe (1950)

Lewis's Major Literary Awards

1956 Carnegie Medal
  The Last Battle

> *"People won't write the books I want, so I have to do it myself."*

Astrid Lindgren

Born: November 14, 1907
Died: January 28, 2002

Pippi Longstocking is a famous book character. Her wild red braids make her easy to recognize. Children love reading about her zany life. Pippi is the invention of children's author Astrid Lindgren. Lindgren wrote many books during her life. She is best known for the Pippi Longstocking books.

Astrid Lindgren was born on November 14, 1907, in Vimmerby, Sweden. Her name then was Astrid Ericsson. She had an older brother and two younger sisters. Astrid's parents were farmers. She once said that she couldn't imagine anyone having more fun than she did growing up.

Astrid remembered what it was like to discover books and to learn to read. "Country girls like me didn't have books . . . after awhile I learned

---

PIPPI LONGSTOCKING HAS BEEN TRANSLATED INTO SIXTY-TWO LANGUAGES.

how to read myself and I was constantly on the hunt for more books to satisfy my hunger for reading. . . . My first book was *Snow White* with on the cover a drawing of a chubby little princess with black curls," Lindgren once said.

In high school, her friends often told her they thought she would be an author one day. Astrid didn't like to hear that. "I think that scared me, I didn't dare try, even though somewhere deep inside I probably thought it would be fun to write," she explained.

> *"It is useless to make a conscious effort to try and recall how things were. You have to relive your own childhood and remember with your very soul what the world looked like."*

In 1923, after graduating from high school, Astrid Lindgren worked for the Vimmerby newspaper. Then, in 1926, she moved to the city of Stockholm, Sweden, to study to be a secretary. Over the next ten years, she married Sture Lindgren and had two children, Lars and Karin.

Astrid Lindgren's children loved hearing their mother's stories about her childhood and growing up on the farm. When Karin was seven, she became ill with pneumonia. She begged her mother to tell her a story. A name popped into Karin's head. "Tell me a story about Pippi Longstocking!" she begged. So Lindgren did. Lindgren and Karin made up many stories about the zany girl named Pippi. But none of them was ever written down.

THERE IS A BRONZE STATUE OF ASTRID LINDGREN IN A PARK
IN STOCKHOLM. THE NAME OF THE PARK IS TENERLUNDEN.

Leo Lionni

Born: May 5, 1910
Died: October 12, 1999

If Leo Lionni had never written a single book, he still would have been a famous man. In his long career, Lionni was a painter, an architecture critic, and a professor of design. He was the art director of several important magazines, which means that he decided how they would look and what sort of pictures they would contain. He displayed his art in galleries and museums in the United States and Europe. Yet when Leo Lionni died and the newspapers wrote about him, the first thing most of them said was that he wrote books for children.

Leo Lionni was born on May 5, 1910, in Amsterdam, the Netherlands. His family was artistic and creative. Leo's mother was an opera singer. He had an uncle who was an architect. Two other uncles were art collectors. They made sure that Leo saw good art.

In school, Leo was mostly interested in nature and art. He kept terrariums filled with animals and plants. He also liked to go to the art museum and copy the pictures and sculptures he saw there.

EVEN THOUGH THE CHARACTERS IN LIONNI'S *LITTLE BLUE AND LITTLE YELLOW* ARE JUST BLOBS OF COLOR, LIONNI SAID CHILDREN ALWAYS GUESS RIGHT WHEN ASKED WHICH BLOB IS LITTLE BLUE'S MOTHER AND WHICH ONE IS HIS FATHER.

The Lionni family moved several times during Leo's childhood, and he lived in Belgium, the United States, and Italy. He returned to the United States to live in 1939 and became a U.S. citizen in 1945.

Leo Lionni's first book for children was written almost by accident. In 1958, he was taking his two grandchildren on a train trip from New York to Connecticut. The children were restless, and their grandfather

> *"I was not a great reader. I don't remember any children's books. I remember books about expeditions to the North Pole and to the South Pole, and I remember reading about penguins."*

A Selected Bibliography of Lionni's Work

An Extraordinary Egg (1994)

On My Beach There Are Many Pebbles (1994)

A Busy Year (1992)

Mr. McMouse (1992)

Matthew's Dream (1991)

Nicolas, Where Have You Been? (1987)

It's Mine! (1986)

Colors to Talk about (1985)

Letters to Talk about (1985)

Numbers to Talk about (1985)

Words to Talk about (1985)

Cornelius: A Fable (1983)

Let's Make Rabbits: A Fable (1982)

Geraldine, the Music Mouse (1979)

In the Rabbitgarden (1975)

Pezzettino (1975)

The Greentail Mouse (1973)

Theodore and the Talking Mushroom (1971)

Fish Is Fish (1970)

Alexander and the Wind-Up Mouse (1969)

The Alphabet Tree (1968)

The Biggest House in the World (1968)

Frederick (1967)

Tico and the Golden Wings (1964)

Swimmy (1963)

Inch by Inch (1960)

Little Blue and Little Yellow: A Story for Pippo and Ann and Other Children (1959)

Lionni's Major Literary Awards

1970 Caldecott Honor Book
  Alexander and the Wind-Up Mouse

1968 Caldecott Honor Book
  Frederick

1964 Caldecott Honor Book
  Swimmy

1961 Caldecott Honor Book
  Inch by Inch

> *"I have a theory that it's impossible not to think in words, and it's impossible not to think in images. I believe we think in both, and it's very difficult to keep them apart. I've tried to do that, and it's like jumping your own shadow."*

tried to entertain them. He tore circles of colored paper from a magazine and made up a story about a little blue blob and a little yellow blob who were friends. The children (and the other passengers!) were delighted. Lionni made his story into a mock-up book and showed it to a book editor. In 1959, it was published as *Little Blue and Little Yellow: A Story for Pippo and Ann and Other Children.* Lionni had begun a new career.

In the 1950s, Little Blue and Little Yellow was unusual. For one thing, its characters were neither people nor animals. They were just blobs. For another, it was created by using collage, an art technique that was unusual in books then.

Lionni created a book almost every year for the rest of his life. Two of his most famous are *Swimmy* and *Frederick.* In *Swimmy,* a school of small red fish fool a big tuna that wants to eat them by making themselves look like an even bigger fish. Swimmy, a little black

CHILDREN LOVE HIS BOOKS, BUT LIONNI ALWAYS HAD A HARD TIME GETTING ALONG WITH CHILDREN HIMSELF. "I DON'T KNOW HOW TO GET TO THEM," HE EXPLAINED. "I WISH I COULD JUST READ TO THEM."

fish, becomes the eye of the make-believe big fish. *Frederick,* like many of Lionni's books, is about a mouse. The plot is a bit like Aesop's fable of the ants and the grasshopper. Frederick the mouse is a poet who helps his friends through the winter with his stories and songs. Art helps the group survive.

Lionni continued to write and paint until the end of his life. He died on October 12, 1999, in Italy.

WHERE TO FIND OUT MORE ABOUT LEO LIONNI

BOOKS

Lionni, Leo. *Between Worlds: An Autobiography of Leo Lionni.*
New York: Knopf, 1997.

Smaridge, Norah. *Famous Author-Illustrators for Young People.*
New York: Dodd, Mead, 1973.

WEB SITES

EDUCATIONAL PAPERBACK ASSOCIATION
http://www.edupaperback.org/authorbios/Lionni_Leo.html
To read a biographical sketch of and a booklist for Leo Lionni

RANDOM HOUSE: AUTHOR BIOS
http://www.randomhouse.com/teachers/rc/rc_ab_lli.html
To read an autobiographical sketch of Leo Lionni

LIONNI DIDN'T THINK CHILDREN'S BOOKS SHOULD BE JUST FOR CHILDREN. "I BELIEVE A GOOD CHILDREN'S BOOK SHOULD APPEAL TO ALL PEOPLE WHO HAVE NOT COMPLETELY LOST THEIR ORIGINAL JOY AND WONDER IN LIFE," HE SAID.

POET

Myra Cohn Livingston

A

CIRCLE

OF

SEASONS

Leonard Everett Fisher

PAINTER

A Selected Bibliography of Livingston's Work

Cricket Never Does: A Collection of Haiku and Tanka (1997)

B Is for Baby: An Alphabet of Verses (1996)

Call Down the Moon: Poems of Music (Selections, 1995)

Animal, Vegetable, Mineral: Poems about Small Things (Selections, 1994)

I Never Told and Other Poems (1992)

Let Freedom Ring: A Ballad of Martin Luther King, Jr. (1992)

Light & Shadow (1992)

Poem-Making: Ways to Begin Writing Poetry (1991)

Birthday Poems (1989)

Up in the Air (1989)

Earth Songs (1986)

A Circle of Seasons (1982)

The Way Things Are, and Other Poems (1974)

The Malibu, and Other Poems (1972)

Wide Awake, and Other Poems (1959)

Whispers, and Other Poems (1958)

published in 1958. She also had other poems published when she was a student.

When she finished college, Livingston returned to California. She worked for several newspapers and wrote book reviews.

She met her husband while visiting Dallas, Texas. After she was married, she lived in Dallas for about thirteen years. Livingston began teaching creative writing there. She taught classes for young people at the public library. She continued to teach creative writing after she and her family moved back to California.

Livingston's poetry is simple and easy to understand. Many of her poems deal with problems that children face. She won lots of awards for her own poetry and for anthologies of other writers' poetry she edited.

Livingston died on August 23, 1996, in Los Angeles, California. She was seventy years old.

"I believe the most important contribution I can make is to guide the young to become aware of their sensitivities and individuality and find a form in which to communicate these strengths to others."

WHERE TO FIND OUT MORE ABOUT MYRA COHN LIVINGSTON

BOOKS

McElmeel, Sharron L. *100 Most Popular Children's Authors: Biographical Sketches and Bibliographies.* Englewood, Colo.: Libraries Unlimited, 1999.

Something about the Author. Autobiography Series. Vol. 1. Detroit: Gale Research, 1986.

Sutherland, Zena. *Children and Books.* New York: Addison Wesley Longman, 1997.

WEB SITES

HARPERCHILDRENS.COM
http://www.harperchildrens.com/catalog/excerpt_xml.asp?isbn=0060240199
To read an excerpt of *Poem-Making* by Myra Cohn Livingston

EVEN AFTER BECOMING A WRITER, LIVINGSTON CONTINUED TO PLAY THE FRENCH HORN. SHE PERFORMED WITH PROFESSIONAL MUSICIANS SEVERAL TIMES THROUGHOUT HER LIFE.

Megan Lloyd

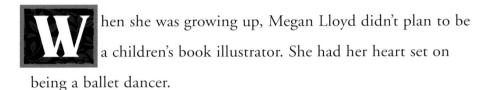

Born: November 5, 1958

When she was growing up, Megan Lloyd didn't plan to be a children's book illustrator. She had her heart set on being a ballet dancer.

Megan took lessons throughout her childhood, and she—along

with everyone else in her family—was sure she would become a professional ballerina. There was just one problem. When she was a teenager, Megan was only five feet, one inch tall. That was much too short to dance professionally. Megan was disappointed, but she soon found a new way to express

LLOYD ENJOYS RESTORING ANTIQUE FURNITURE.

herself. She became an artist.

Megan Lloyd was born on November 5, 1958, in Harrisburg, Pennsylvania. Her father and mother were both teachers. The family also included Megan's older sister, as well as a dog and a cat. The family was close and active, and they enjoyed sharing activities such as horseback riding.

Megan was fifteen years old when she realized that she would never be a professional ballet dancer. So she focused her creative energies on the visual arts instead. Luckily, her high school had an excellent art department. Megan's teachers

"Each book presents a new puzzle to solve."

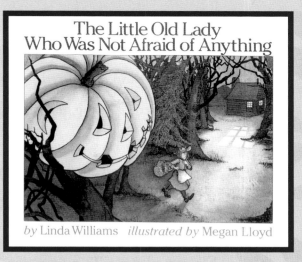

The Little Old Lady Who Was Not Afraid of Anything

by Linda Williams   *illustrated by* Megan Lloyd

A Selected Bibliography of Lloyd's Work

Fancy That! (2003)

Thanksgiving at the Tappletons' (2003)

Horse in the Pigpen (2002)

Heeey, Ma! (2002)

Pioneer Church (1999)

Chirping Crickets (1998)

Falcons Nest on Skyscrapers (1996)

Too Many Pumpkins (1996)

Dance with Me (1995)

Winter Wheat (1995)

The Perfectly Orderly House (1994)

The Gingerbread Doll (1993)

The Gingerbread Man (1993)

Lobster Boat (1993)

The Christmas Tree Ride (1992)

How You Talk (1992)

Look Out for Turtles! (1992)

Baba Yaga: A Russian Folktale (1991)

Cactus Hotel (1991)

Super Cluck (1991)

How We Learned the Earth Is Round (1990)

That Sky, That Rain (1990)

The Little Old Lady Who Was Not Afraid of Anything (1988)

More Surprises (1987)

The Atlantic Free Balloon Race (1986)

Farmer Mack Measures His Pig (1986)

All Those Mothers at the Manger (1985)

Surprises (1984)

Chicken Tricks (Text and illustrations, 1983)

Arnold Lobel

Born: May 22, 1933
Died: December 4, 1987

Arnold Lobel wanted to use his books for children to teach important lessons. Some of his most famous books are about Frog and Toad. He used these two funny characters to teach children about how to be a good friend.

Lobel has written and illustrated many other books for children. His best-known books include A Holiday for Mister Muster, Frog and Toad All Year, Days with Frog and Toad, and Ming Lo Moves the Mountain.

Arnold Lobel was born on May 22, 1933, in Los Angeles, California. Shortly after he was born, Arnold and his family moved to Schenectady, New York.

MUCH OF LOBEL'S INSPIRATION FOR HIS BOOKS CAME FROM REMEMBERING HIS OWN CHILDHOOD AND FROM OBSERVING THE CARTOONS HIS OWN CHILDREN LIKED TO WATCH.

When he was in kindergarten, first, and second grades, Arnold was sick a lot. He missed many days of school because he was in the hospital or at home. It was hard for him to make friends because he was not in school very much.

By the time Arnold was in third grade, he was healthier. He used his interest in drawing and storytelling to make friends. He

> *"Somehow in the writing of the manuscript for* **Frog and Toad** *I was, for the first time, able to write about myself. Frog and Toad are really two aspects of myself."*

had drawn many pictures on the days that he was not in school. When he returned to school, he shared his pictures with his new friends. His friends loved to hear Arnold's stories, too.

When he entered high school, Arnold decided that he wanted to become an artist. He studied the illustrations of many artists. He wanted to learn how other artists did their work.

When he graduated from high school, he attended art school in Brooklyn, New York. Lobel met his wife at the school. She also became an author and illustrator of children's books.

While he attended art school, Lobel lived in an apartment near the zoo. He often went to the zoo to draw pictures of the animals. His many trips to the zoo inspired him to write and illustrate his first

LOBEL NEVER LIKED TO USE THE SAME TECHNIQUE
TO ILLUSTRATE DIFFERENT BOOKS. INSTEAD, HE PREFERRED TO
VARY HIS STYLE DEPENDING ON THE TONE OF THE MANUSCRIPT.

Thomas Locker

Born: June 26, 1937

Thomas Locker's two favorite things in the world are art and nature. Throughout his career as a painter and children's book illustrator, he has been able to combine these two loves to create beauty in several different forms.

Thomas Locker was born on June 26, 1937, in New York City. His father was a political lobbyist, and his mother was a book dealer. Although Thomas lived in the city, he made many visits to the country, too. He soon learned to love the beauty of the countryside, which was so different from his city home.

Locker graduated from the University of Chicago in 1960. He went on to receive a master of fine arts degree from American Univer-

---

LOCKER DISCOVERED ILLUSTRATED CHILDREN'S BOOKS
WHILE READING TO HIS FIVE SONS.

sity in Washington, D.C.

Although Locker loved to paint, his first job was as a teacher. From 1963 to 1973, he was a professor of art at several colleges in the Midwest. Locker continued to paint during his years as a college professor.

By 1973, Thomas Locker had shown his paintings at art galleries all around the United States. That year, Locker made a big decision: He left teaching and became a full-time artist.

During the 1960s and 1970s, Locker was also busy raising a family. He married Marea Panares Teske in 1964. The couple had a son, Anthony, before they divorced in 1971.

Then Locker married

WHERE THE RIVER BEGINS
by Thomas Locker

A Selected Bibliography of Locker's Work

Mountain Dance (2001)

Cloud Dance (2000)

In Blue Mountains: An Artist's Return to America's First Wilderness (2000)

Grandfather's Christmas Tree (Illustrations only, 1999)

Water Dance (1997)

Between Earth & Sky: Legends of Native American Sacred Places (Illustrations only, 1996)

The Earth Under Sky Bear's Feet: Native American Poems of the Land (Illustrations only, 1995)

Sky Tree: Seeing Science through Art (1995)

To Climb a Waterfall (Illustrations only, 1995)

Anna and the Bagpiper (1994)

The First Thanksgiving (Illustrations only, 1993)

The Ice Horse (Illustrations only, 1993)

Calico and Tin Horns (Illustrations only, 1992)

Thirteen Moons on Turtle's Back: A Native American Year of Moons (Illustrations only, 1992)

Catskill Eagle (Illustrations only, 1991)

The Land of Gray Wolf (1991)

Snow toward Evening: A Year in River Valley: Nature Poems (Illustrations only, 1990)

The Young Artist (1989)

Family Farm (1988)

Washington Irving's Rip Van Winkle (1988)

The Boy Who Held Back the Sea (Illustrations only, 1987)

The Ugly Duckling (Illustrations only, 1987)

Sailing with the Wind (1986)

The Mare on the Hill (1985)

Miranda's Smile (1984)

Where the River Begins (1984)

Lois Lowry

Born: March 20, 1937

A rebellious girl dealing with the humorous troubles of everyday life. A teenager coping with her older sister's fatal illness. A young girl fighting against the Nazis during World War II. A boy who struggles to fit into a controlling society. These compelling characters all spring from the creative mind of one author, Lois Lowry.

Lois Lowry was born on March 20, 1937, in Honolulu, Hawaii. Her maiden name is Lois Hammersberg. Her father was an army dentist. During World War II (1939–1945), her father served with the U.S. Army while Lois, her mother, her older sister, and her younger brother lived with Lois's grandparents in Pennsylvania. Lois missed her father terribly during those years. She was thrilled when the family was finally reunited after the war.

LOWRY SPENT PART OF HER CHILDHOOD IN TOKYO, JAPAN, WHILE HER FATHER WAS STATIONED THERE WITH THE ARMY.

Lois always loved books. She learned to read at the age of three. When she started school, Lois preferred to sit alone with a book rather than join her classmates in playing games.

Lois was only sixteen when she graduated from high school. She was determined to be a writer, and she enrolled at Brown University in Rhode Island in 1954. However, she dropped out of school after only two years when she married a naval officer named Donald Grey Lowry. The couple had four children before they divorced in 1977.

Although Lowry enjoyed being a wife and mother, she was unhappy about having to drop out of school to raise a family. Finally, in 1972, Lowry was able to complete her education. She received a degree from the University of Southern Maine. While she was in school, she and her children did their homework together at the kitchen table.

> *"The most important things to me in my own life, as well as in my books, are human relationships of all kinds."*

During the 1970s, Lowry's short stories began appearing in magazines. She also wrote several literature textbooks. Then, in 1977, Lowry published her first novel, *A Summer to Die.* This book tells the story of a thirteen-year-old girl who must face the death of her older sister and rival. The novel received excellent reviews, and Lowry's career as a children's book author was born.

––––

LOWRY SKIPPED TWO GRADES IN SCHOOL AND WAS USUALLY THE YOUNGEST AND SMALLEST STUDENT IN HER CLASS.

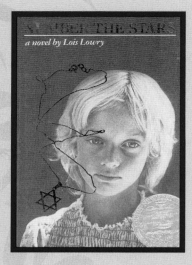

A Selected Bibliography of Lowry's Work

Gooney Bird Greene (2002)
Gathering Blue (2000)
Zooman Sam (1999)
Looking Back: A Book of Memories (1998)
Stay! Keeper's Story (1998)
See You Around, Sam (1996)
Anastasia, Absolutely (1995)
The Giver (1993)
Attaboy, Sam! (1992)
All about Sam (1988)
Number the Stars (1989)
Anastasia's Chosen Career (1987)
Rabble Starkey (1986)
Anastasia, Ask Your Analyst (1984)
The One Hundredth Thing about Caroline (1983)
Taking Care of Terrific (1983)
Anastasia Again! (1981)
Autumn Street (1980)
Anastasia Krupnik (1979)
Find a Stranger, Say Goodbye (1978)
A Summer to Die (1977)

Lowry's Major Literary Awards

1994 Newbery Medal
1993 *Boston Globe–Horn Book* Fiction Honor Book
　The Giver

1990 Newbery Medal
　Number the Stars

1987 *Boston Globe–Horn Book* Fiction Award
　Rabble Starkey

Lowry wrote many kinds of books during the next twenty-five years. Some of her books, such as *Rabble Starkey,* are serious, but she wrote humorous stories as well. Perhaps Lowry's most popular works are the books about Anastasia Krupnik. These stories focus on a spunky preteen girl who faces everyday problems such as troublesome parents, the embarrassments of gym class, and the arrival of a baby brother.

> *"I think, in general, anybody who wants to write anything should a, read a lot and b, write a lot, and quit worrying about who's going to buy it."*

During the 1990s, Lowry became one of the most respected authors for young readers. In 1990, her book *Number the Stars* won the prestigious Newbery Medal as the best children's novel of the year. *Number the Stars* looks at life under the Nazis from a child's point of view. In 1994, Lowry won her second Newbery Medal for *The Giver,* a science-fiction novel about a futuristic society.

Today, Lowry lives in New England. She enjoys her family—which now includes several grandchildren—and continues to write funny, tragic, haunting, and always compelling stories about young people in the world.

∿

WHERE TO FIND OUT MORE ABOUT LOIS LOWRY

BOOKS

Hill, Christine M. *Ten Terrific Authors for Teens.* Berkeley Heights, N.J., 2000.

Lowry, Lois. *Looking Back: A Book of Memories.* Boston: Houghton Mifflin, 1998.

McElmeel, Sharron L. *100 Most Popular Children's Authors: Biographical Sketches and Bibliographies.* Englewood, Colo.: Libraries Unlimited, 1999.

WEB SITES

EDUCATIONAL PAPERBACK ASSOCIATION
http://www.edupaperback.org/authorbios/Lowry_Lois.html
To read an autobiographical sketch of and a booklist for Lois Lowry

THE INTERNET PUBLIC LIBRARY
http://www.ipl.org/youth/AskAuthor/Lowry.html
To read an autobiographical sketch of Lois Lowry and the transcript of an interview

LOWRY TOOK THE PHOTOGRAPH THAT APPEARS ON THE COVER OF *THE GIVER.*

David Macaulay

Born: December 2, 1946

David Macaulay uses words and pictures to show and tell how the everyday objects around us work. His books explore how buildings are built and how wheels go around. Macaulay's drawings for each book are as entertaining as they are informative. If readers look at the drawings closely, they will find small stories unfolding in each scene. Macaulay hopes these images will stay with his readers.

David Macaulay was born on December 2, 1946, in Burton-on-Trent, England. His father worked on machines for the textile industry. As a boy, David watched his father working on do-it-yourself projects around the house. He, too, became interested in the inner workings of things. He began building cardboard models of

SEVERAL OF MACAULAY'S BOOKS HAVE BEEN TURNED INTO TELEVISION SERIES.

skyscrapers, complete with elevators that he could raise and lower with a string.

Macaulay also fondly remembers the long walk through woods to his school. He liked to daydream and let his imagination roam free during the walk.

David and his family moved to the United States when he was eleven. In high school, he discovered that his talent for drawing could make him popular. He won friends by making drawings of the Beatles and other stars.

After graduation from high school, David Macaulay attended the Rhode Island School of Design, where he studied architecture. However, he never

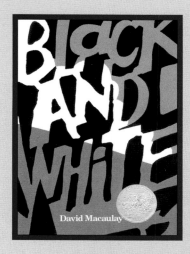

A Selected Bibliography of Macaulay's Work

Angelo's Work (2002)
Building Big (2000)
Building the Book Cathedral (1999)
The New Way Things Work (1998)
Why the Chicken Crossed the Road (1997)
Black and White (1990)
The Way Things Work (1988)
Baaa (1985)
Unbuilding (1980)
Motel of the Mysteries (1979)
Great Moments in Architecture (1978)
Castle (1977)
Underground (1976)
Pyramid (1975)
City: A Story of Roman Planning and Construction (1974)
Cathedral: The Story of Its Construction (1973)

Macaulay's Major Literary Awards

1991 Caldecott Medal
   Black and White

1989 *Boston Globe–Horn Book* Nonfiction Honor Book
   The Way Things Work

1978 *Boston Globe–Horn Book* Nonfiction Honor Book
1978 Caldecott Honor Book
   Castle

1976 *Boston Globe–Horn Book* Nonfiction Honor Book
   Pyramid

1974 Caldecott Honor Book
   Cathedral: The Story of Its Construction

worked as an architect. Instead, he worked at a number of jobs, including teaching junior-high art.

His first book began as a story about a beauty pageant for gargoyles—the scary mythological creatures carved on the walls of cathedrals. Editors at one publishing company liked his drawings for the book, but they didn't like the beauty pageant story. Instead, Macaulay changed the book so that it told how a cathedral was built. *Cathedral: The Story of Its Construction* was published in 1973. It won several awards, including one as the best illustrated children's book of the year.

Over the next seven years, Macaulay produced a different book each year. His second book was *City: A Story of Roman Planning and Construction.* It took readers on a tour of an ancient Roman city. *Pyramid* explored the huge monuments to ancient Egyptian pharaohs. *Castle* revealed the inner workings of a medieval European fortress.

In 1988, Macaulay published *The Way Things Work.* His detailed drawings

> *"I want to communicate. . . . For me the point is to leave a picture in somebody's mind—not necessarily a sentence or a paragraph. . . ."*

> *"We create all these things and then we think of ourselves as too stupid to understand them. . . . I hope [my work] says to readers, 'You can figure it out.'"*

Some of Macaulay's drawings are in the collections of art museums, including the Cooper Hewitt Museum and the Toledo Museum of Art.

and clear writing helped readers understand even the most complicated gadgets. The book shows what makes cars run, how nail clippers clip, and the scientific principle behind a seesaw.

Despite his complex subjects, Macaulay makes his books entertaining and humorous. He lives with his family in Providence, Rhode Island.

❧

WHERE TO FIND OUT MORE ABOUT DAVID MACAULAY

BOOKS

McElmeel, Sharron L. *100 Most Popular Picture Book Authors and Illustrators: Biographical Sketches and Bibliographies.* Englewood, Colo.: Libraries Unlimited, 2000.

Norby, Shirley, and Gregory Ryan. *Famous Illustrators of Children's Literature.* Minneapolis: T. S. Denison, 1992.

Something about the Author.
Vol. 46. Detroit: Gale Research, 1987.

WEB SITES

BUILDING BIG: LIVE CHAT WITH DAVID MACAULAY
http://www.pbs.org1wgbh/buildingbig/chat.html
To read a live chat transcript with Macaulay

HOUGHTON MIFFLIN: BIOGRAPHY OF DAVID MACAULAY
http://www.houghtonmifflinbooks.com/features/davidmacaulay/bio.htm
To read a biographical sketch of David Macaulay, a booklist, and book reviews

———

MACAULAY CONSIDERS HIMSELF FIRST AND FOREMOST AN ILLUSTRATOR.

Patricia MacLachlan

Born: March 3, 1938

Patricia MacLachlan is an award-winning author of picture books and novels for children. She is best known as the author of *Sarah, Plain and Tall.* MacLachlan's other books include *The Sick Day, The Facts and Fictions of Minna Pratt,* and *Arthur, for the Very First Time.*

Patricia MacLachlan was born on March 3, 1938, in Cheyenne, Wyoming. She was an only child and had a close relationship with her parents. Both of her parents were teachers. She read many books by herself and with her family. "We read them, discussed them, reread them and acted out the parts," MacLachlan remembers.

As a young girl, Patricia did not write stories, but she used her imagination to create fantasies about Mary, an imaginary

ACTRESS GLENN CLOSE STARRED IN THE
TELEVISION PRODUCTION OF *SARAH, PLAIN AND TALL.*

friend of hers. MacLachlan notes that "Mary was real enough for me to insist that my parents set a place for her at the table." Her parents encouraged Patricia to use her imagination.

Patricia and her family moved to Minnesota for a few years before she went on to college. She attended the University of Connecticut. After she graduated, she taught English. She also got married and had three children.

> *"I feel it's crucial that kids who aspire to write understand that I have to rewrite and revise as they do. Ours is such a perfectionist society—I see too many kids who believe that if they don't get it right the first time, they aren't writers."*

MacLachan then began working at a social-service agency while she was still raising her own children at home. At the agency, MacLachlan worked with foster mothers. She wrote a series of journal articles about adoption and foster mothers. These are themes that later became important in her writing for children. "It was clear to me that much of the focus of my writing was sharpened by my involvement and concern for families and children," MacLachlan says.

As her children grew older and entered school, MacLachlan felt she needed to do something else. "It dawned on me that what I really wanted to do was to write," she recalls. MacLachlan began her career as a children's author by writing picture books. Before she wrote her first book,

MacLachlan didn't begin her
writing career until she was thirty-five years old.

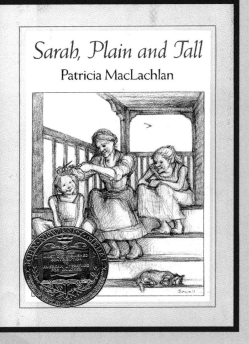

Sarah, Plain and Tall
Patricia MacLachlan

A Selected Bibliography of MacLachlan's Work

Painting the Wind (2003)
Caleb's Story (2001)
All the Places to Love (1994)
Skylark (1994)
Baby (1993)
Journey (1991)
The Facts and Fictions of Minna Pratt (1988)
Sarah, Plain and Tall (1985)
Unclaimed Treasures (1984)
Cassie Binegar (1982)
Tomorrow's Wizard (1982)
Arthur, for the Very First Time (1980)
The Sick Day (1979)

MacLachlan's Major Literary Awards

1986 Newbery Medal
1986 Scott O'Dell Award
   Sarah, Plain and Tall
1984 *Boston Globe–Horn Book* Nonfiction Honor Book
   Unclaimed Treasures

MacLachlan read hundreds of children's books. Her first book, *The Sick Day*, was published in 1979.

After writing several picture books, MacLachlan was encouraged by her editor to write novels for young people. Her first novel, *Arthur, for the Very First Time,* was published in 1980. She found that picture books were more difficult to write than a novel. "A good picture book is much like a poem," MacLachlan notes.

In her books, MacLachlan writes about things that happen in everyday life. "My books derive chiefly from my family life, both as a child with my own parents as well as with my husband and kids," MacLachan says. She believes that young people can relate better to things that could and do happen to them.

> *"Writing for children is special because I think children read with a great true belief in what they're reading."*

Along with writing, MacLachlan teaches a course on children's literature at Smith College. She gives lectures on writing and visits schools to talk about her books with children. She also gives writing workshops for children. MacLachlan lives with her family in Massachusetts, where she continues to write.

❧

WHERE TO FIND OUT MORE ABOUT PATRICIA MACLACHLAN

BOOKS

McElmeel, Sharron L. *100 Most Popular Children's Authors: Biographical Sketches and Bibliographies.* Englewood, Colo.: Libraries Unlimited, 1999.

Silvey, Anita, ed. *Children's Books and Their Creators.* Boston: Houghton Mifflin, 1995.

WEB SITES

EDUCATIONAL PAPERBACK ASSOCIATION
http://www.edupaperback.org/authorbios/Maclachlan_Patricia.html
To read a biographical sketch of and a booklist for Patricia MacLachlan

RANDOM HOUSE: AUTHORS/ILLUSTRATORS
http://www.randomhouse.com/teachers/authors/macl.html
To read a biographical sketch of Patricia MacLachlan, as well as a message from the author

———

THE CHARACTERS AUNT ELDA AND UNCLE WRISBY, WHO APPEAR IN THE BOOK *ARTHUR, FOR THE VERY FIRST TIME,* ARE MODELED AFTER MACLACHLAN'S MOTHER AND FATHER.

Margaret Mahy

Born: March 21, 1936

Margaret Mahy's job as a librarian helped her to be a better writer. "Being a librarian certainly helped me even more with my writing because it made me even more of a reader," Mahy says. After working as a librarian, Mahy went on to become a children's author. Her most popular books include *The Haunting; The Changeover: A Supernatural Romance; The Tricksters;* and *Memory.*

Margaret Mahy was born on March 21, 1936, in Whakatane, New Zealand. She is the oldest of five children. Her father would tell the children stories and read to them. Her father's stories of adventure inspired Margaret to become a writer.

Margaret had one of her stories published in a newspaper when she was seven years old. She

MARGARET MAHY HAS A VERY OLD CAT NAMED ORSINO. IT SLEEPS ON HER FAX MACHINE BECAUSE IT IS ALWAYS WARM!

also entered many of her stories in writing contests.

Margaret had a happy childhood. Many of her family's relatives lived in the same town. She loved to spend time with her family, who were very important to her. When she became a writer, she often wrote about family life.

In high school, Margaret was a very good student. She was also a very good swimmer. When she finished high school, she worked as a nurse's aide for six months. She then went on to college.

"Being a writer is what I have most wanted to be, from the time I was a child."

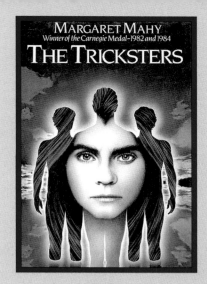

A Selected Bibliography of Mahy's Work

Dashing Dog (2002)
Down the Dragon's Tongue (2000)
Twenty-Four Hours (2000)
Simply Delicious! (1999)
Don't Read This! And Other Tales of the Unnatural (1998)
Boom, Baby, Boom, Boom (1997)
Busy Day for a Good Grandmother (1995)
My Mysterious World (1995)
The Catalogue of the Universe (1994)
The Pirate Uncle (1994)
Dangerous Spaces (1991)
The Door in the Air and Other Stories (1991)
The Seven Chinese Brothers (1990)
Memory (1988)
The Tricksters (1986)
Aliens in the Family (1985)
The Haunting (1982)
The Boy Who Was Followed Home (1975)
Ultra-Violet Catastrophe (1975)
The Changeover: A Supernatural Romance (1974)
A Lion in the Meadow (1969)

Mahy's Major Literary Awards

1988 *Boston Globe–Horn Book* Fiction Honor Book
   Memory
1985 *Boston Globe–Horn Book* Fiction Honor Book
1984 Carnegie Medal
   The Changeover: A Supernatural Romance
1982 Carnegie Medal
   The Haunting

Mahy studied at college to become a librarian. She found a job as a librarian when she finished college. She worked at many different

> *"A very short, simple story that works well is just as exciting to me as any longer and more complex book."*

libraries in New Zealand and England before becoming a full-time writer in 1980.

While she was working as a librarian, Mahy wrote poems and stories. She tried to get her writing published by companies in New Zealand. She had a few stories published there in the early 1960s.

Mahy became more successful when her first book was published in the United States. The book, *A Lion in the Meadow,* was published in 1969. Mahy went on to have many more of her picture books, novels, nonfiction books, and book series published throughout the world.

Mahy writes for many different age groups of children. "I don't think I prefer writing for one age group above another," Mahy notes. "I am just as pleased with a story which I feel works well for very small children as I am with a story for young adults." In her writing, Mahy often uses humor. She also writes about real issues that young people may experience.

> *"I have told children all the truth I know from personal experience."*

MAHY'S STORIES HAVE BEEN TRANSLATED INTO FIFTEEN LANGUAGES.

Mahy continues to write for children and young people. She lives with her family in Governor's Bay, New Zealand.

❧

WHERE TO FIND OUT MORE ABOUT MARGARET MAHY

BOOKS

Kovacs, Deborah, and James Preller. *Meet the Authors and Illustrators: 60 Creators of Favorite Children's Books Talk About Their Work.* Vol. 1. New York: Scholastic, 1991.

Mahy, Margaret. *My Mysterious World.*
Katonah, N.Y.: R.C. Owen, 1995.

WEB SITES

CHRISTCHURCH CITY LIBRARIES

http://library.christchurch.org.nz/Childrens/MargaretMahy/about.asp#MMawards
To read a biographical sketch of Margaret Mahy, a booklist, and a selection of awards

THE SCOOP

http://www.friend.ly.net/scoop/biographies/mahymargaret/index.html
To read an autobiographical sketch of Margaret Mahy

MAHY WROTE MANY SCRIPTS FOR NEW ZEALAND
TELEVISION, INCLUDING *THE MARGARET MAHY STORY
BOOK THEATRE, CUCKOOLAND,* AND *A LAND CALLED HAPPY.*

James Marshall

Born: October 10, 1942
Died: October 13, 1992

James Marshall is remembered for being a talented artist. He was dedicated to the business of children's books, and he had a passion for his work. *George and Martha* was the first of more than thirty-five books written and illustrated by Marshall.

James Marshall was born on October 10, 1942, in San Antonio, Texas. He grew up on a farm sixteen miles outside of the city. James's father had a dance band, and his mother sang in the church choir. Coming from this musical family, James planned to become a violist. He even won a scholarship to attend the New England Conservatory of Music. But he injured his hand during an airplane trip and had to change his plans.

SUBSTITUTE TEACHER VIOLA SWAMP IN THE MISS NELSON
BOOKS IS BASED ON MARSHALL'S SECOND-GRADE TEACHER,
WHO HAS SEEN THE BOOKS AND THINKS THEY'RE FUNNY.

Marshall attended Trinity University back home in Texas. His French teacher was Harry Allard. The two men later worked together on several series of books. Marshall finished college at Southern Connecticut State College, where he earned a degree in history and French. He got a job teaching Spanish and French at a high school in Boston—even though he had to learn Spanish as he went along.

While he was teaching, Marshall resumed his old hobby of drawing. (He had given it up back in second grade when a teacher laughed at him.) A friend introduced him to a book editor, and Marshall was given his first assign-

> *"People have very odd ideas of what a children's writer should be like. Children always expect me to look like a hippopotamus and adults assume that by nature I have to be a little off the wall."*

ment. He got the job of illustrating *Plink, Plink, Plink* by Byrd Baylor, which was published in 1971.

Next, Marshall came up with a story of his own. *George and Martha*, published in 1972, is the tale of two hippos. It was the first of seven stories about these hippo friends. Years later, when all the George and Martha stories were collected in one volume, it was 340 pages long.

Marshall had several popular series of books in addition to the George and Martha books. The books in the Stupids series, several of

MARSHALL ONCE HAD A DREAM IN WHICH MARTHA COMPLAINED ABOUT HIS STORIES. SHE WANTED BETTER LINES—AND IF SHE DIDN'T GET THEM, SHE THREATENED TO GO TO ANOTHER ILLUSTRATOR'S HOUSE.

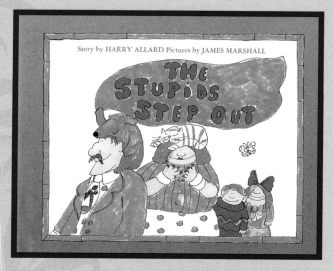

Story by HARRY ALLARD Pictures by JAMES MARSHALL

THE STUPIDS STEP OUT

A Selected Bibliography of Marshall's Work

James Marshall's Cinderella (Illustrations only, 2001)

Eugene (2000)

Swine Lake (1999)

The Owl and the Pussycat (Illustrations only, 1998)

George and Martha: The Complete Stories about Two Best Friends (1997)

Pocketful of Nonsense (1993)

The Cut-Ups Crack Up (1992)

Rats on the Roof and Other Stories (1991)

The Stupids Take Off (with Harry Allard, 1989)

Goldilocks and the Three Bears (1988)

Red Riding Hood (1987)

The Stupids Die (Illustrations only, 1981)

The Cut-Ups (1984)

Troll Country (1980)

Portly McSwine (1979)

Miss Nelson Is Missing! (with Harry Allard, 1977)

Mary Alice, Operator Number 9 (Illustrations only, 1975)

The Stupids Step Out (Illustrations only, 1974)

George and Martha (1972)

Plink, Plink, Plink (Illustrations only, 1971)

Marshall's Major Literary Awards

1999 *Boston Globe–Horn Book* Picture Book Honor Book
  The Owl and the Pussycat

1989 Caldecott Honor Book
  Goldilocks and the Three Bears

which he wrote with Allard, were about a family so foolish that (in one book) when the lights go out they think they've all died. The Cut-Ups books told the adventures of two wild boys, Joe and Spud, and their battle against the cranky school principal, Lamar J. Spurgle. There was also a series of books about a young fox, which Marshall wrote under the name Edward Marshall. For awhile, Marshall pretended that Edward was a peculiar cousin of his from Texas. He also wrote adaptations of fairy tales and illustrated books by many other authors.

Marshall's style of drawing was extremely simple. His friend Maurice Sendak compared him with great illustrators such as

Randolph Caldecott and Jean de Brunhoff (who wrote and illustrated the Babar books). Sendak pointed to a picture in which Martha the hippo is planning a trick on George. "How did Marshall convey dementia, malice and get-evenness with two mere flicks of his pen for eyes?" he wondered.

> *"A book must have a good beginning and a strong middle, but without a knock-out ending, you're shot."*

Marshall was a funny, lively man who loved food and music and friendship. Sendak called him "a wicked angel" for his wit and warmth. He died on October 13, 1992, at the age of fifty.

❧

Where to Find Out More about James Marshall

Books

De Montreville, Doris, and Elizabeth D. Crawford, eds. *Fourth Book of Junior Authors & Illustrators.* New York: H. W. Wilson Company, 1978.

Kovacs, Deborah, and James Preller. *Meet the Authors and Illustrators: 60 Creators of Favorite Children's Books Talk about Their Work.* Vol. 2. New York: Scholastic, 1993.

Web Sites

Carol Hurst's Children's Literature Site
http://www.carolhurst.com/newsletters/42enewsletters.html
To read a biographical sketch of James Marshall and descriptions of some of his books

University of Southern Mississippi de Grummond Collection
http://www.lib.usm.edu/~degrum/findaids/marshall.htm
To read a biographical sketch of and a booklist for James Marshall

———

WHILE MARSHALL WAS CREATING HIS FAMOUS HIPPOS, EDWARD ALBEE'S PLAY *WHO'S AFRAID OF VIRGINIA WOOLF?* WAS ON TELEVISION. THE PLAY IS ABOUT AN UNHAPPY COUPLE NAMED GEORGE AND MARTHA.

books about a babysitting cooperative. The editor asked Martin to write four books for the series. The books were popular, and Martin was asked to write two more books for the series. Those books were very popular, too, and many copies were sold. "That was when we decided that we really had something," Martin says.

Martin is the author of almost all the books in the Baby-Sitters Club and Baby-Sitters Little Sister series. When she first began writing the series, she would write two books each month. She now has other authors help her write books for the series.

"I write books as pure entertainment for myself, as well as for the kids, but I hope that avid readers . . . are reading other things, too, and I also hope that reluctant readers who get hooked on reading through series reading . . . will then 'graduate' to other kinds of books."

Currently Martin, writes three-quarters of the books published each year in both series. Even though she does not write all the books, she outlines the chapters of each book. She also edits the books before they are published.

In her writing, Martin relies on her memory. She can remember things that happened to her as a young girl. She uses these memories in her books. "When I speak through my young characters, I am remembering and reliving," she notes. "Redoing all those things one is never supposed to be able to redo."

MARTIN BASED THE BOOK *STAGE FRIGHT* ON HER OWN STAGE FRIGHT SHE EXPERIENCED AS A CHILD.

Along with her writing, Martin is active in supporting community programs. She also supports a dance program at an elementary school in New York City. She continues to write books and lives with her pets in Upstate New York.

> *"I think one has to keep in mind exactly what kids are going to be getting out of the books. Children, no matter what anybody thinks, are very vulnerable."*

WHERE TO FIND OUT MORE ABOUT ANN M. MARTIN

BOOKS

Kovacs, Deborah, and James Preller. *Meet the Authors and Illustrators: 60 Creators of Favorite Children's Books Talk about Their Work.* Vol. 2. New York: Scholastic, 1993.

WEB SITES

KIDSREADS.COM
http://www.kidsreads.com/authors/au-martin-ann.asp
To read a biographical sketch of Ann M. Martin

SCHOLASTIC ONLINE AUTHORS
http://www.scholastic.com/annmartin/index.htm
To read letters from Ann M. Martin to her fans

MARTIN HAD MANY PETS WHEN SHE WAS A CHILD. AT ONE POINT, NINE CATS WERE LIVING AT HER HOUSE!

Bill Martin Jr.

Born: March 20, 1916

For nearly six decades, Bill Martin Jr. has crafted hundreds of books that are hits with parents and kids alike. What makes his books so good? Martin chooses each and every word carefully. He speaks his sentences aloud before he writes them down, making sure that each one has the perfect rhythm and the best possible sound. Martin's careful choice of words has helped to make him one of the most successful and popular children's picture book authors.

William Ivan Martin was born on March 20, 1916, in Hiawatha, Kansas. Even though there weren't many books around the house when Bill was growing up, he heard lots of great stories. Bill's parents and his grandmother were all excellent storytellers. Bill was fascinated by their magical tales.

MARTIN HAS APPEARED ON TWO EDUCATIONAL TELEVISION SERIES: *STORY TELLER* (1955) AND *BILL MARTIN* (1968).

In elementary school, Bill's love of listening continued. His favorite teacher, Miss Davis, read to her students constantly. Even when story time was over, Miss Davis would continue reading if her students asked her to.

Although Bill loved listening to stories, he didn't like to read them. Martin says he was a nonreader until he went to college.

> *"A blessed thing happened to me when I was a child. I had a teacher who read to me."*

There, with the help of caring teachers, the young man learned the joys of reading. Martin's favorite things to read were poems. He memorized works by Stephen Vincent Benét and Robert Frost, repeating them aloud to others. Martin graduated from college and began teaching high school journalism, drama, and English classes.

During World War II (1939–1945), Martin entered the air force. He served as a newspaper reporter and got his first writing experience. When Martin returned to Kansas, he and his brother Bernard decided to team up and create a children's book. *Little Squeegy Bug* featured words by Bill and pictures by Bernard. When they couldn't find a publisher for the book, the two brothers published their work themselves. Over the next eight years, they wrote and published seventeen books together.

Martin went back to college in Chicago to learn more about children and reading. While he was studying, he also worked as an elementary

WILLIAM IVAN MARTIN WAS NAMED FOR BOTH HIS FATHER (WILLIAM) AND HIS MOTHER (IVA). IN COLLEGE, WHEN BILL WOULDN'T REVEAL HIS MIDDLE NAME, HE WAS LISTED AS BILL MARTIN JR. THE NAME STUCK.

Bill Martin Jr / Eric Carle

Polar Bear, Polar Bear, What Do You Hear?

A Selected Bibliography of Martin's Work

Little Granny Quarterback (with Michael Sampson, 2001)
Rock It, Sock It, Number Line (with Michael Sampson, 2001)
Chicken Chuck (with Bernard Martin, 2000)
A Beasty Story (with Steven Kellogg, 1999)
Swish! (with Michael Sampson, 1997)
Polar Bear, Polar Bear, What Do You Hear? (1991)
Chicka Chicka Boom Boom (with John Archambault, 1989)
The Magic Pumpkin (with John Archambault, 1989)
Knots on a Counting Rope (with John Archambault, 1987)
Barn Dance! (with John Archambault, 1986)
White Dynamite & Curly Kidd (with John Archambault, 1986)
The Ghost-Eye Tree (with John Archambault, 1985)
Here Are My Hands (with John Archambault, 1985)
Brown Bear, Brown Bear, What Do You See? (1970)
Little Squeegy Bug (with Bernard Martin, 1945)

Martin's Major Literary Awards

1990 *Boston Globe–Horn Book* Picture Book Honor Book
  Chicka Chicka Boom Boom

school principal. In 1961, Martin moved to New York City to become a textbook editor. As an editor, he helped create reading, social studies, science, and math programs for kids.

When Martin began to write full-time, his love of listening helped him out. Martin has a good ear for fun words and fine language. He knows a terrific story when he tells one, too. Today, Martin still says that he doesn't write books—he speaks them.

One of Martin's most famous books is *Brown Bear,*

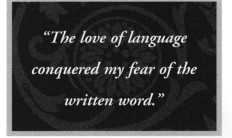

"The love of language conquered my fear of the written word."

Brown Bear, What Do You See? Martin got the idea for Brown Bear when he was riding on a train. By the time the thirty-minute trip was over, he had planned the entire book in his head.

Today, Martin lives in Commerce, Texas. When he's not writing, he likes to sing folk songs. Martin also travels around the nation, giving speeches to young and old who admire his gift as a master storyteller.

❧

WHERE TO FIND OUT MORE ABOUT BILL MARTIN JR.

BOOKS

Kovacs, Deborah, and James Preller. *Meet the Authors and Illustrators: 60 Creators of Favorite Children's Books Talk about Their Work.* Vol. 2. New York: Scholastic, 1993.

WEB SITES

BILL MARTIN JR. AND MICHAEL SAMPSON WEB SITE
http://www.tiill.com/bill.htm
To read a biographical sketch of Bill Martin Jr. and information about his books

THE SCOOP
http://www.friend.ly.net/scoop/biographies/martinbill/index.html
To read the transcript of an interview with Bill Martin Jr.

—————

THE BILL MARTIN JR. LIBRARY IS LOCATED AT TEXAS A&M UNIVERSITY IN COMMERCE, TEXAS. THE LIBRARY, WHICH OPENED IN SEPTEMBER 2000, HOLDS MANY OF MARTIN'S BOOKS, MANUSCRIPTS, AND LETTERS.

Mercer Mayer

Born: December 10, 1943

Mercer Mayer was born on December 30, 1943, in Little Rock, Arkansas, while his father was serving in World War II (1939–1945). Mercer was already about two years old when he first met his father. Mercer's father was in the U.S. Navy, so the family moved many times. Mercer and his family finally settled in Hawaii.

As a young boy, Mercer loved to draw. He enjoyed looking at illustrated books, too. "I was in love with the world, or should I say worlds, they depicted," Mayer remembers. "Pen and ink was always quite magical for me and still is. I was amazed that a bottle

---

MAYER IS ONE OF THE FIRST AUTHORS TO CREATE WORDLESS PICTURE BOOKS.

of black ink and a scratchy pen point could create such wonderful things."

After graduating from high school, Mercer Mayer went to the Honolulu Academy of Arts. His art instructors were impressed with his talent, but they discouraged him from becoming a book illustrator.

In 1964, Mayer moved to New York City to continue his art studies. He was still interested in working as a book illustrator.

"Now I'm a big kid and I write about things that happen now, especially with my own children. They always remind me of what it was like."

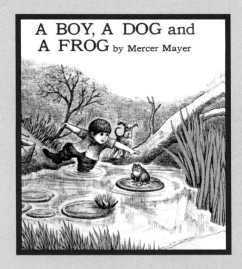

A Selected Bibliography of Mayer's Work

The Mixed-Up Morning (2002)
Camping Out (2001)
Helping Mom (2001)
Little Critter's the Best Present (2000)
Just a Bully (with Gina Mayer, 1999)
The Figure in the Shadows (Illustrations only, 1993)
Thrills and Spills (1991)
Appelard and Liverwurst (1978)
Little Monster's Neighborhood (1978)
Everyone Knows What a Dragon Looks Like (Illustrations only, 1976)
Liza Lou and the Yeller Belly Swamp (1976)
Professor Wormbog in Search of the Zipperump-a-Zoo (1976)
The Great Cat Chase: A Wordless Book (1975)
Just for You (1975)
Frog Goes to Dinner (1974)
Two More Moral Tales (1974)
Walk, Robot, Walk (1974)
What Do You Do with a Kangaroo? (1974)
You're the Scaredy-Cat (1974)
Frog on His Own (1973)
A Silly Story (1972)
The Queen Always Wanted to Dance (1971)
A Special Trick (1970)
Frog, Where Are You? (1969)
I Am a Hunter (1969)
There's a Nightmare in My Closet (1968)
If I Had . . . (1968)
Terrible Troll (1968)
A Boy, a Dog and a Frog (1967)

He showed his portfolio of drawings to many publishers, but he was not able to find a job. "Finally I received some good advice from an art director," Mayer says. "He told me to throw my portfolio away because it was so bad."

Mayer was disappointed, but he decided to take the advice. He found a job with an advertising agency and worked on improving his illustration skills.

After his skills improved, Mayer was asked to illustrate several children's books. He also created drawings for his own first book, *A Boy, a Dog and a Frog*. This book was published in 1967. It was a picture book that did not include any words. Mayer also used words in many of the books that he has created since that time.

"Most of my books are about things that happened to me when I was a little kid," Mayer explains. He writes stories and creates illustrations from a child's point of view. This style makes his books more interesting to children. Some of his best-known books are in the Little Critter and Little Monster series.

Mayer continues to work on writing and illustrating his own books. He also

> *"I didn't really want to be an artist. Originally, I wanted to be an astronomer—actually, I wanted to ride a UFO and go to Mars."*

MAYER DESCRIBES HIS CHILDHOOD AS BEING VERY MUCH LIKE THE CHILDHOOD OF TOM SAWYER, THE FICTIONAL CHARACTER CREATED BY MARK TWAIN.

finds time to illustrate books written by other authors.

Mercer Mayer has four children and lives in Connecticut. "It's real fun to be an old kid," says Mayer.

❧

WHERE TO FIND OUT MORE ABOUT MERCER MAYER

BOOKS

De Montreville, Doris, and Elizabeth D. Crawford, eds. *Fourth Book of Junior Authors & Illustrators.* New York: H. W. Wilson Company, 1978.

McElmeel, Sharron L. *100 Most Popular Picture Book Authors and Illustrators: Biographical Sketches and Bibliographies.* Englewood, Colo.: Libraries Unlimited, 2000.

Silvey, Anita, ed. *Children's Books and Their Creators.* Boston: Houghton Mifflin, 1995.

WEB SITES

EDUCATIONAL PAPERBACK ASSOCIATION
http://www.edupaperback.org/authorbios/Mayer_Mercer.html
To read an autobiographical sketch of and a booklist for Mercer Mayer

THE OFFICIAL LITTLE CRITTER WEB SITE
http://www.littlecritter.com/
To read about the Little Critter characters, view an online movie, and access coloring pages related to the series

---

MAYER HAS ALWAYS BEEN FASCINATED BY
BLACK-AND-WHITE PEN-AND-INK DRAWINGS.

Robert McCloskey

Born: September 15, 1914

Robert McCloskey is well known for his children's books about real-life people and places. Three of his best-known books are *Make Way for Ducklings, Homer Price,* and *Blueberries for Sal.* But McCloskey didn't plan on being a writer. Before writing children's books, he had many other interests.

Robert McCloskey was born on September 15, 1914, in Hamilton, Ohio. As a child, he loved music. He began by taking piano lessons. Soon, he was also playing harmonica, oboe, and drums.

Robert also developed an interest in mechanical things. He wanted to know how machines worked. He tried his own mechanical inventions.

McCloskey was the first person to win two Caldecott Medals.

As he got older, Robert discovered art. He began drawing for his high school newspaper. He was so good that he won a scholarship to study at Boston's Vesper George School of Art after high school. At that point, it seemed that McCloskey would focus on a career as an artist. He continued to study art at the National Academy of Design in New York and privately with an artist on Cape Cod, Massachusetts.

> *"It is just sort of an accident that I write books. I really think up stories in pictures and just fill in the pictures with a sentence or a paragraph or a few pages of words."*

McCloskey received some advice from a children's book editor in New York. McCloskey showed her drawings he had done of characters from fantasy and mythology. She was not very impressed. She suggested that he focus on the things in the real world. He needed to pay attention to what went on around him and to center his art on real characters and events.

During the next several years, McCloskey took her advice. He wrote a book about a boy who played the harmonica. This boy could have been McCloskey himself! The book was called *Lentil* and was published in 1940.

Make Way for Ducklings was McCloskey's next book. It took him almost three years to complete it. It was important that he draw and

McCloskey got the idea for *Make Way for Ducklings* when he was living in Boston and saw real ducks getting in the way of traffic around the Boston Public Garden.

MAKE WAY FOR DUCKLINGS

Robert McCloskey

A Selected Bibliography of McCloskey's Work

Burt Dow, Deep-Water Man: A Tale of the Sea in the Classic Tradition (1963)

Time of Wonder (1957)

Journey Cake, Ho! (1953)

One Morning in Maine (1952)

Centerburg Tales (1951)

Blueberries for Sal (1948)

Homer Price (1943)

Make Way for Ducklings (1941)

Lentil (1940)

McCloskey's Major Literary Awards

1958 Caldecott Medal
Time of Wonder

1954 Caldecott Honor Book
Journey Cake, Ho

1953 Caldecott Honor Book
One Morning in Maine

1949 Caldecott Honor Book
Blueberries for Sal

1942 Caldecott Medal
Make Way for Ducklings

write about the ducks accurately. So one day he bought four live ducks. He brought them home and followed them around his apartment for the next few weeks.

Many of McCloskey's books are based on real people and on events in his own life. *Homer Price* gave McCloskey an opportunity to think back on his childhood experiences in the Midwest. In *Blueberries for Sal,* McCloskey based the main character, Sal, on his daughter Sarah. The sequel, *One Morning in Maine,* includes a character, Jane, based on his second daughter. Her name is Jane, too. Both stories reflect the McCloskey family's experiences living in Maine.

McCloskey's books are known for their heartwarming stories and illustrations. He feels strongly about the role of art both in his books and in the world of children. McCloskey says "It is important that we develop people who can make worthwhile pictures, and it is important that we teach people to 'read' these pictures. That is why, in my opinion, every child, along with learning to read and write, should be taught to draw and to design."

> *"I get a lot of letters. Not only from children but from adults, too. Almost every week, every month, clippings come in from some part of the world where ducks are crossing the street."*

WHERE TO FIND OUT MORE ABOUT ROBERT McCLOSKEY

BOOKS

Collier, Laurie, and Joyce Nakamura, eds. *Major Authors and Illustrators for Children and Young Adults.* Detroit: Gale Research, 1993.

Kovacs, Deborah, and James Preller. *Meet the Authors and Illustrators: 60 Creators of Favorite Children's Books Talk about Their Work.* Vol. 1. New York: Scholastic, 1991.

WEB SITES

EDUCATIONAL PAPERBACK ASSOCIATION
http://www.edupaperback.org/authorbios/McCloskey_Robert.html
To read an autobiographical sketch of and a booklist for Robert McCloskey

THE SCOOP
http://www.friend.ly.net/scoop/biographies/mccloskeyrobert/
To read a biographical sketch of and a booklist for Robert McCloskey

LARGER-THAN-LIFE BRONZE STATUES OF McCLOSKEY'S MOTHER DUCK AND DUCKLINGS WERE PLACED IN THE BOSTON PUBLIC GARDEN IN HONOR OF McCLOSKEY'S AWARD-WINNING BOOK.

McCully studied art history at Brown University in Rhode Island. She later earned a master's degree from Columbia University in New York City. After college, she got a job working in an advertising agency. When this didn't seem like it was going to turn into a career, she showed some of her drawings to art directors at publishing houses. Gradually, she began getting jobs designing covers for books.

Then one day, an editor saw a poster she had made hanging in a New York City subway station. The editor tracked her down and asked her if she wanted to illustrate a book. It was *Sea Beach Express,* written by George Panetta, and it was the beginning of her career in children's books. Since then, McCully has illustrated about 200 books for other authors, including *How to Eat Fried Worms,* by Thomas Rockwell, and *Black Is Brown Is Tan,* by Arnold Adoff.

> *"My advice for aspiring artists and writers is this: Don't worry about what other people are doing. . . . Work from what is inside you, crying out—however softly, however timidly— for expression."*

McCully did not create a children's book of her own until 1984, almost twenty years after she began illustrating other people's books. Called *Picnic,* it is a wordless book about a family of mice. Since then, McCully has written many easy-reader books, including *Grandmas at Bat* and *The Grandma Mix-Up: Stories and Pictures.* But most often, she writes for older children.

ALL OF BELLINI'S HIGH-WIRE FEATS IN MCCULLY'S BOOKS ARE BASED ON THOSE OF A REAL HIGH-WIRE WALKER NAMED BLONDIN. BLONDIN EVEN COOKED EGGS WHILE STANDING ON A WIRE STRETCHED ACROSS NIAGARA FALLS.

McCully enjoys writing about historical subjects. *The Bobbin Girl* is about a ten-year-old working in a textile factory in the early 1800s, and *The Orphan Singer* is about a girl who becomes a famous singer in eighteenth-century Italy. As long as McCully keeps coming across interesting historic characters, she will always have material for more books.

> *"Part of the courage it takes to be an author—or to do anything worth doing—is to risk rejection and to risk failure."*

WHERE TO FIND OUT MORE ABOUT EMILY ARNOLD McCULLY

BOOKS
Silvey, Anita, ed. *Children's Books and Their Creators.*
Boston: Houghton Mifflin, 1995.

Sutherland, Zena. *Children and Books.*
New York: Addison Wesley Longman, 1997.

WEB SITES
BALTIMORE COUNTY PUBLIC LIBRARY
http://www.bcplonline.org/kidspage/mccully.html
To read a biographical sketch of and a booklist for Emily Arnold McCully

SCHOLASTIC ONLINE
http://www2.scholastic.com/teachers/authorsandbooks/authorstudies/authorhome.jhtml?authorID=59&collateralID=5230&displayName=Biography
To read an autobiographical sketch, a booklist, and the transcript of an interview with Emily Arnold McCully

THOUGH McCULLY IS FAMOUS FOR THE WATERCOLOR PAINTINGS IN HER BOOKS, SHE ONLY BEGAN PAINTING IN 1992. BEFORE THAT, SHE ALWAYS DREW PICTURES WITH A PEN AND THEN FILLED IN THE COLOR.

Gerald McDermott

Born: January 31, 1941

Gerald McDermott wanted to be a filmmaker. He studied filmmaking for several years, and he even made several films for children that were successful. He was then asked to create books for children from stories in his films. Since then, he has written and illustrated several books from his films. His best-known books include *The Magic Tree: A Tale from the Congo*, *The Stonecutter: A Japanese Folk Tale*, and *The Knight of the Lion*.

Gerald McDermott was born on January 31, 1941, in Detroit, Michigan. When Gerald was about four years old, his parents noticed his talent for art. He was very good at drawing and painting pictures. They enrolled him in art classes at the Detroit Institute of Arts. He attended classes every Saturday until he was a teenager.

McDERMOTT'S FILM *ANANSI THE SPIDER* WON THE 1970 AMERICAN FILM FESTIVAL BLUE RIBBON.

When he was nine years old, Gerald appeared on a radio show. He was one of the actors in a folktale performance. This experience taught Gerald many things. He learned about the technical parts of doing a performance. He also learned how to work with actors. This experience was helpful to him when he became a filmmaker later in life.

Gerald attended a high school in Detroit that had a special arts curriculum. He studied art, music, and dance. He wanted to study filmmaking, but the school did not have any film courses. So he began to make films on his own. He also got a part-time job creating backgrounds for a television animation studio.

In 1959, McDermott won a scholarship to attend an art school in New York. But this school did not have any courses in filmmaking, either. Instead of going to school, McDermott took a job as a graphic designer for a television station. He went back to school about one year later. For the next several years, McDermott spent most of his time making films for children. All his films were animated and took a great deal of time to create.

> *"Every Saturday, from early childhood through early adolescence, was spent in those halls [in the Detroit Institute of Arts]. I virtually lived in the museum, drawing and painting and coming to know the works of that great collection. I've kept a brush in my hand ever since."*

McDERMOTT'S ANIMATED FILMS REQUIRED HIM TO DRAW **6,000** INDIVIDUAL PICTURES. THE PICTURES— OR FRAMES—WERE FILMED AND ACCOMPANIED BY MUSIC.

A Selected Bibliography of McDermott's Work

Jabutí the Tortoise: A Trickster Tale from the Amazon (2001)

The Fox and the Stork (1999)

Musicians of the Sun (1997)

Raven: A Trickster Tale from the Pacific Northwest (1993)

Zomo the Rabbit: A Trickster Tale from West Africa (1992)

Marcel the Pastry Chef (Illustrations only, 1991)

Tim O'Toole and the Wee Folk: An Irish Tale (1990)

Daniel O'Rourke: An Irish Tale (1986)

Daughter of Earth: A Roman Myth (1984)

Carlo Collodi's The Adventures of Pinocchio (Illustrations only, 1981)

Papagayo: The Mischief Maker (1980)

The Knight of the Lion (1979)

The Voyage of Osiris: A Myth of Ancient Egypt (1977)

The Stonecutter: A Japanese Folk Tale (1975)

Arrow to the Sun: A Pueblo Indian Tale (1974)

The Magic Tree: A Tale from the Congo (1973)

Anansi the Spider: A Tale from the Ashanti (1972)

McDermott's Major Literary Awards

1994 Caldecott Honor Book

1993 *Boston Globe–Horn Book* Picture Book Honor Book
   Raven: A Trickster Tale from the Pacific Northwest

1975 Caldecott Medal
   Arrow to the Sun: A Pueblo Indian Tale

1973 *Boston Globe–Horn Book* Picture Book Honor Book
   The Magic Tree: A Tale from the Congo

1973 Caldecott Honor Book
   Anansi the Spider: A Tale from the Ashanti

McDermott enjoyed making films, but he was discouraged because he was not making much money. He and his wife, an author and illustrator of children's books, decided to move to France. Before they moved, he met with his wife's publisher. McDermott was hired to create children's books from his movies. McDermott found this to be an interesting

"It has been my experience that even the youngest children respond in a direct and receptive manner to the most stylized of images. I believe this quality is manifested in the magic and symbolism of their own paintings."

challenge. This began a new career for McDermott as a children's book author and illustrator. His first book, *Anansi the Spider: A Tale from the Ashanti,* was published in 1972. He has since written and illustrated several other children's books based on folktales.

McDermott continues to write and illustrate books for children and young people. He lives with his wife in New York.

❧

WHERE TO FIND OUT MORE ABOUT GERALD McDERMOTT

BOOKS

De Montreville, Doris, and Elizabeth D. Crawford, eds. *Fourth Book of Junior Authors & Illustrators.* New York: H. W. Wilson Company, 1978.

WEB SITES

GERALD McDERMOTT'S READING ROOM
http://showcase.netins.net/web/reading/juvmcd.html
To read synopses of some of Gerald McDermott's books

GERALD McDERMOTT'S WEB SITE
http://www.geraldmcdermott.com/
To read a biographical sketch of Gerald McDermott,
and for information about his books

———

MANY OF McDERMOTT'S BOOKS HAVE BEEN PUBLISHED IN JAPAN.
HE HAS TRAVELED THROUGHOUT JAPAN GIVING SPEECHES ABOUT HIS WORK.

Megan McDonald

Born: February 28, 1959

Author Megan McDonald knows what it's like to have some bad days. Growing up with four bossy older sisters, Megan definitely had a few. But Megan's childhood experiences came in handy when she began creating fiction stories for children. Her strong and sassy kid characters and their amazing adventures attract readers of all ages.

Megan McDonald was born on February 28, 1959, in Pittsburgh, Pennsylvania. Her father was an ironworker, and her mother was a social worker. Megan and her sisters grew up surrounded by books and stories.

Megan's father was a great storyteller who would make up stories about anything—even designs he saw in the

---

McDONALD HAS HAD MANY PETS, INCLUDING SNAKES, TURTLES, AND NEWTS.

peanut butter or the ice cream. At dinner, Megan, her parents, and her sisters would gather in the kitchen to swap stories about their day.

As the youngest child, Megan had a tough time getting a word in edgewise. To give her the chance to freely express herself, Megan's mother bought her a journal to write in.

Although Megan's sisters took control of the talking, they also introduced her to the world of books. They taught her to check the end of a book first to make sure she wanted to read the whole thing. If the ending made Megan cry, then the book was worth reading. Megan's sisters also let her tag along when the bookmobile was in the

A Selected Bibliography of McDonald's Work
Penguin and Little Blue (2003)
Judy Moody Saves the World (2002)
Judy Moody Gets Famous (2001)
Reptiles Are My Life (2001)
Beezy and Funnybone (2000)
Lucky Star (2000)
Shadows in the Glasshouse (2000)
Bedbugs (1999)
The Bone Keeper (1999)
Insects Are My Life (1999)
Judy Moody (1999)
The Night Iguana Left Home (1999)
Beezy at Bat (1998)
Beezy Magic (1998)
Beezy (1997)
Tundra Mouse: A Storyknife Tale (1997)
My House Has Stars (1996)
The Bridge to Nowhere (1993)
The Great Pumpkin Switch (1992)
Whoo-oo Is It? (1992)
The Potato Man (1991)
Is This a House for Hermit Crab? (1990)

neighborhood. Megan always checked out the same book, a biography of Virginia Dare. Finally, Megan was banned from taking out the book so that other kids could have the chance to read it.

"What I like about writing is that in all things there is a story—a leaf falling, . . . a child on the way to school, a stranger on the bus, something found in the street. One begins to see differently, and each new thing takes on an aspect of story."

As a teenager, Megan enjoyed books and stories. When she was fourteen, Megan worked at a local library. As an adult, she took jobs that kept her connected to books and to children. Over the years, McDonald has worked as a librarian, a park ranger, a museum guide, and a storyteller. She put her first story on paper in 1990, when she completed *Is This a House for Hermit Crab?* Four years later, McDonald left her job as a librarian and began writing full-time.

McDonald gets many of the ideas for stories from her own memories and experiences. Both the Beezy books and the Judy Moody books, for example, feature events from McDonald's childhood. When McDonald wrote the first Judy Moody book, she used herself as the model for the title character. But McDonald made Judy the oldest so that she could finally have a shot at being the boss!

Some of McDonald's books are based on stories her father told her

MCDONALD WAS IN THE FIFTH GRADE WHEN SHE WROTE
HER FIRST STORY. CALLED "THE PLEA OF THE PENCIL SHARPENER,"
THE STORY WAS ABOUT LIFE FROM A PENCIL SHARPENER'S POINT OF VIEW.

and her sisters when they were young. *The Potato Man* and *The Great Pumpkin Switch* are two such books. They are based on tales about her father's childhood in Pittsburgh during the Great Depression.

> *"Connecting children with books has always been the centerpiece of my life's work."*

One of McDonald's favorite things about being a writer is to put herself into her characters' shoes. She enjoys spending the day thinking like a mouse or like a girl from colonial times. McDonald says she can get an idea from just about anything.

McDonald lives in California with her husband, Richard. She enjoys visiting schools, where she tells stories and talks about her books.

❧

WHERE TO FIND OUT MORE ABOUT MEGAN MCDONALD

BOOKS

Holtze, Sally Holmes, ed. *Seventh Book of Junior Authors & Illustrators.*
New York: H. W. Wilson Company, 1996.

WEB SITES

FABLE VISION
http://www.fablevision.com/judymoody/mmcdonald.html
For a biographical sketch and a photo of Megan McDonald

VISITINGAUTHORS.COM
http://visitingauthors.com/authors/mcdonald_megan/mcdonald_megan_bio.html
To read a biographical sketch of and a booklist for Megan McDonald

———

IN ONE OF MCDONALD'S BOOKS, SHE INVENTED A CREATURE CALLED A PRICKLEPINE FISH. MCDONALD HAS RECEIVED LETTERS FROM KIDS ACROSS THE COUNTRY SAYING THAT THEY'VE SPOTTED THIS MAKE-BELIEVE ANIMAL.

A Selected Bibliography of McKissack's Work

Days of Jubilee: The End of Slavery in the United States (with Fredrick McKissack, 2003)

Black Hands, White Sails: The Story of African-American Whalers (with Fredrick McKissack, 1999)

Rebels against Slavery: American Slave Revolts (with Fredrick McKissack, 1996)

Christmas in the Big House, Christmas in the Quarters (with Fredrick McKissack, 1994)

The Dark-Thirty: Southern Tales of the Supernatural (1992)

Madam C. J. Walker: Self-Made Millionaire (with Fredrick McKissack, 1992)

Sojourner Truth: Ain't I a Woman? (with Fredrick McKissack, 1992)

Carter G. Woodson: The Father of Black History (with Fredrick McKissack, 1992)

W.E.B. DuBois (with Fredrick McKissack, 1990)

A Long Hard Journey: The Story of the Pullman Porter (with Fredrick McKissack, 1989)

Flossie & the Fox (1986)

Paul Laurence Dunbar: A Poet to Remember (1984)

McKissack's Major Literary Awards

2000 Carter G. Woodson Honor Book
2000 Coretta Scott King Author Honor Book
  Black Hands, White Sails: The Story of African-American Whalers

1997 Coretta Scott King Author Honor Book
  Rebels against Slavery: American Slave Revolts

1995 Coretta Scott King Author Award
1995 Orbis Pictus Honor Book
  Christmas in the Big House, Christmas in the Quarters

1995 Coretta Scott King Author Honor Book
  Black Diamond: The Story of the Negro Baseball Leagues

1993 *Boston Globe–Horn Book* Nonfiction Award
1993 Coretta Scott King Author Honor Book
  Sojourner Truth: Ain't I a Woman?

1993 Carter G. Woodson Book Award
  Madam C. J. Walker: Self-Made Millionaire

1993 Coretta Scott King Author Award
1993 Newbery Honor Book
  The Dark-Thirty: Southern Tales of the Supernatural

1992 Carter G. Woodson Outstanding Merit Book
  Carter G. Woodson: The Father of Black History

1991 Carter G. Woodson Outstanding Merit Book
  W.E.B. DuBois

1990 Carter G. Woodson Outstanding Merit Book
1990 Coretta Scott King Author Award
  A Long Hard Journey: The Story of the Pullman Porter

American society.

In 1975, McKissack earned a master's degree in early childhood literature from Webster University in Saint Louis, Missouri. She has been a junior high school English teacher and a part-time college instructor. Through her teaching, she has tried to inspire her students with her own love of literature.

McKissack has also written highly praised fictional tales with realistic black characters as well as stories about country mice and city mice. Her stories are notable for their depiction of human emotion. Her tales are often inspired by her childhood in the South.

> *"Writing has allowed us to do something positive with our experiences, although some of our experiences have been very negative. We try to enlighten, to change attitudes, to form new attitudes—to build bridges with books."*

Patricia McKissack's fiction and nonfiction are charged with a sense of pride and history. McKissack seems to have lived up to Kennedy's challenge, giving something back to society and helping to shape a better one.

WHERE TO FIND OUT MORE ABOUT PATRICIA MCKISSACK

BOOKS

Kovacs, Deborah, and James Preller. *Meet the Authors and Illustrators: 60 Creators of Favorite Children's Books Talk about Their Work.* Vol. 2. New York: Scholastic, 1993.

McElmeel, Sharron L. *100 Most Popular Children's Authors: Biographical Sketches and Bibliographies.* Englewood, Colo.: Libraries Unlimited, 1999.

WEB SITES

CHILDREN'S LITERATURE: MEET THE AUTHORS AND ILLUSTRATORS
http://www.childrenslit.com/f_mckissack.html
To read a biographical sketch of Patricia McKissack and short descriptions of some of her books

---

MCKISSACK IS A MEMBER OF THE METHODIST CHURCH. SHE HAS INCORPORATED RELIGIOUS THEMES INTO SEVERAL BOOKS, INCLUDING *WHEN DO YOU TALK TO GOD?* AND *PRAYERS FOR SMALL CHILDREN*.

Eve Merriam

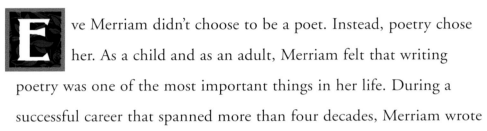

Born: July 19, 1916
Died: April 11, 1992

Eve Merriam didn't choose to be a poet. Instead, poetry chose her. As a child and as an adult, Merriam felt that writing poetry was one of the most important things in her life. During a successful career that spanned more than four decades, Merriam wrote hundreds of poems for children and grown-ups alike. She wrote about serious subjects and silly subjects, from poverty and crime to vanilla ice cream and umbrellas. Merriam also created picture books and nonfiction works for kids as well as books and plays for adults.

Eve Merriam was born on July 19, 1916, in Philadelphia, Pennsylvania. Her mother and father were Russian immigrants.

MERRIAM WAS ALSO A GIFTED PLAYWRIGHT. HER PLAYS, SOME OF WHICH SHE PRODUCED AND DIRECTED, HAVE BEEN PERFORMED ON BROADWAY AND IN THEATERS ACROSS THE COUNTRY.

They owned a dress shop in Philadelphia, which sparked Eve's lifelong interest in fashion. The youngest of four children, Eve had two older sisters and an older brother.

Growing up, Eve learned to love the sound of poetry spoken aloud. She was drawn to its rhythm and rhyme. Eve loved the way every single word in a poem is important. Some of the first poems Eve read aloud were printed in her local newspaper. These poems encouraged her to create her own verses, and she composed one of her first poems when she was just seven.

Eve wrote about everything and anything. One of her early poems was about a birch tree outside her window. A line of the

A Selected Bibliography of Merriam's Work

Low Song (2001)
On My Street (2000)
Emma Lazarus Rediscovered (1998)
Bam, Bam, Bam (1995)
Quiet, Please (1993)
The Singing Green: New and Selected Poems for All Seasons (1992)
A Poem for a Pickle: Funnybone Verses (1989)
You Be Good & I'll Be Night: Jump-on-the-Bed Poems (1988)
Blackberry Ink: Poems (1985)
Finding a Poem (1970)
It Doesn't Always Have to Rhyme (1964)
There Is No Rhyme for Silver (1962)
A Gaggle of Geese (1960)
The Real Book about Franklin D. Roosevelt (1952)

> *"I find it difficult to sit still when I hear poetry or read it out loud. I feel a tingling feeling all over, particularly in the tips of my fingers and in my toes, and it just seems to go right from my mouth all the way through my body."*

poem read, "May my life be like the birch tree reaching upward to the sky."

As an adult, Merriam moved to New York City and began a career as a writer. She wrote advertisements, radio scripts, feature stories, and fashion articles. At the same time, she continued to pen her poems.

Her first success as a poet came in 1946. That year, Merriam won an award from Yale University for the most promising young poet. Yale also published her first book, a collection of adult poems called *Family Circle.*

In 1952, Merriam wrote her first children's book—a biography titled *The Real Book about Franklin D. Roosevelt.* After her two sons were born, Merriam became interested in creating other quality books for kids. Her first picture book, *A Gaggle of Geese,* was published in 1960. With its use of wild and wacky words, the book demonstrated Merriam's love for the English language.

In 1962, Merriam published *There Is No Rhyme for Silver,* her first collection of children's poetry. Kids loved Merriam's poems, and more volumes of verse quickly followed.

FOR AWHILE, MERRIAM HAD HER OWN WEEKLY SHOW ON
A NEW YORK CITY RADIO STATION, IN WHICH SHE DISCUSSED MODERN POETRY.

Over the years, Merriam wrote more than twenty poetry books for children. Along the way, she built a reputation as one of the best children's poets of her time. Merriam's poems are fun to read, and they create a love of reading and language in kids.

On April 11, 1992, Merriam died of cancer. Her poems and picture books live on, however. Today, children everywhere continue to enjoy Merriam's amazing work.

> *"As far back as I can remember, I have been intrigued by words: their sound, sight, taste, smell, touch, for it has always seemed to me that they appeal to all the senses."*

WHERE TO FIND OUT MORE ABOUT EVE MERRIAM

BOOKS

Berger, Laura Standley, ed. *Twentieth-Century Young Adult Writers.* 1st ed. Detroit: St. James Press, 1994.

Sutherland, Zena. *Children and Books.* New York: Addison Wesley Longman, 1997.

WEB SITES

THE AMERICAN ACADEMY OF POETS
http://www.poets.org/poets/poets.cfm?prmID=160
To learn more about Eve Merriam's life and work

UNIVERSITY OF SOUTHERN MISSISSIPPI DE GRUMMOND COLLECTION
http://www.lib.usm.edu/~degrum/findaids/merriam.htm
To read a biographical sketch of and a booklist for Eve Merriam

———

WHILE MERRIAM WAS IN COLLEGE, SHE SLEPT WITH A COPY
OF HER FAVORITE BOOK OF POETRY UNDERNEATH HER PILLOW
TO MAKE SURE THAT NO ONE STOLE THE BOOK.

A. A. Milne

Born: January 18, 1882
Died: January 31, 1956

A. Milne spent most of his career as a writer producing plays. Most of his plays, written for an adult audience, were first performed in the 1920s in theaters in London, England, and New York City. Even though Milne wrote only four children's books, he is best known for his work as a children's author. He wrote *Winnie-the-Pooh* and *The House at Pooh Corner.* The characters in these books went on to become favorites of children and adults throughout the world.

Alan Alexander (A. A.) Milne was born on January 18, 1882, in London. Alan's father owned a private school near their home. Alan attended school there until he

MILNE HAD THE HABIT OF SOLVING CROSSWORD
PUZZLES IN THE EVENING AFTER DINNER.

won a scholarship to the Westminster School. He then went on to Cambridge University.

A. A. Milne was a very good student and worked hard. He studied mathematics at the university. He was the editor of the college magazine.

Milne graduated from college in 1903 and began his career as a writer. He became known for humorous essays and plays. His essays were published in a British humor magazine called *Punch*. In 1906, he was offered a job as an assistant editor at *Punch*. He worked at the magazine for eight years.

In 1913, Milne married Dorothy de Selincourt. When World War I (1914–1918) began, he joined the British army. While he was training for service in the army, Milne wrote his first play, *Wurzel-Flummery*. By 1920, Milne had completed one book and several plays. He was very successful and made money from his writing. Milne's only son, Christopher Robin, was born in 1920.

> *"A pen-picture of a child which showed it as loving, grateful, and full of thought for others would be false to the truth; but equally false would be a picture which insisted on the brutal egotism of the child, and ignored the physical beauty which softens it."*

Milne wrote his first children's book while taking a break from writing plays. A friend was starting a magazine for children and asked

---

DISNEY HAS PRODUCED SEVERAL MOVIES OF THE POOH STORIES.

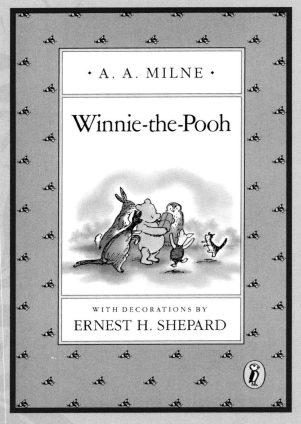

A Selected Bibliography of Milne's Work

him to write a few verses for the publication. As Milne watched his son play, he wrote the verses. The poems were published in Milne's first children's book, *When We Were Very Young.*

In 1926, Milne published the first of two books of short stories about Winnie-the-Pooh. His book *The House at Pooh Corner* was published in 1928. He also wrote another book of poetry, *Now We Are Six,* in 1927.

Milne's poetry and short stories were about his son and his own memories as a child. "My father was a creative writer and so it was precisely because he was not able to play with his small son that his longings sought and found satisfaction in another direction," Christopher Milne later noted. "He wrote about him instead."

The children's books that Milne wrote helped him to relive his own childhood. A. A. Milne continued to write essays, novels, and poetry until his death on January 31, 1956.

"It has been my good fortune as a writer that what I have wanted to write has for the most part proved to be saleable."

❧

WHERE TO FIND OUT MORE ABOUT A. A. MILNE

BOOKS

Toby, Arlene. *A. A. Milne: Author of Winnie-the-Pooh.*
Chicago: Children's Press, 1995.

Ward, S. *Meet A. A. Milne.*
New York: PowerKids Press, 2001.

Wheeler, Jill. *A. A. Milne.* Edina,
Minn.: Abdo & Daughters, 1992.

WEB SITES
POOH CORNER
http://www.pooh-corner.com/biomilne.html
For a biographical sketch of A. A. Milne and information
on the Pooh series and characters

WINNIETHEPOOH.COM
http://www.winniethepooh.co.uk/author.html
To read a biographical sketch of A. A. Milne, descriptions
of Pooh and his friends, and stories and poems by the author

─────

WINNIE-THE-POOH HAS BEEN TRANSLATED INTO
FRENCH, SPANISH, AND SEVERAL OTHER LANGUAGES.

Christopher A. Myers

Born: October 17, 1974

Christopher A. Myers got his start by working with a collaborator—the famous African-American poet and writer Walter Dean Myers. Walter is Christopher's father. The two produced several books together, but really the partnership began much earlier.

"My father was always working on something which he would ask me to research, mostly African-American and labor history," Christopher Myers explains. "For example, my uncle worked in the coal mines of West Virginia. There was an accident. He would have died in the mine shaft had not a woman come by and heard his cries for help. She stayed with him for three days in the mine shaft

———

CHRISTOPHER MYERS AND HIS FATHER, WALTER DEAN MYERS, WORKED ON *HARLEM: A POEM* SEPARATELY, EACH PURSUING HIS OWN IDEAS. "WE'VE GOT DIFFERENT VISIONS," CHRISTOPHER EXPLAINS.

until he got better. Later she became my aunt."

Christopher Myers was born in New York City on October 17, 1974, and has been drawing since he was a child. In fact, he enrolled at an art school at the age of thirteen.

For college, he attended Brown University in Providence, Rhode Island. Myers majored in American history and art semiotics—the study of how images create meaning. After graduation, Myers took part in the American Art Independent Studio Program, a special program for artists run by the Whitney Museum in New York.

Because his father writes children's books, Myers had

A Selected Bibliography of Myers's Work

A Time to Love: Tales from the Old Testament (Illustrations only, 2002)

Fly (2001)

Wings (2000)

Black Cat (1999)

Monster (Illustrations only, 1999)

This I Know: Poetry across Black Cultures (Illustrations only, 1998)

Harlem: A Poem (Illustrations only, 1997)

Galápagos: Islands of Change (1995)

Shadow of the Red Moon (Illustrations only, 1995)

Forest of the Clouded Leopard (Text only, 1994)

Turnip Soup (Text only, 1994)

McCrephy's Field (Text only, 1991)

Myers's Major Literary Awards

2000 Coretta Scott King Illustrator Honor Book
   Black Cat

1999 *Boston Globe–Horn Book* Fiction Honor Book
   Monster

1998 Caldecott Honor Book
1998 Coretta Scott King Illustrator Honor Book
1997 *Boston Globe–Horn Book* Fiction Honor Book
   Harlem: A Poem

"Every time my family gets together, it's Harlem that's on their minds. . . . Harlem is a very different place now . . . but it's still the place that has formed a lot of who I am. I see ways now that . . . Harlem is a legacy, Harlem is an attitude."

long been thinking about them. He felt that many children's books talked down to young readers. He wanted to change that. He also felt that African-Americans needed to see images and pictures that related to them.

Myers's first illustration project was for his father's science-fiction book *Shadow of the Red Moon,* which was published in 1995. The two also worked together on *Harlem: A Poem,* a picture book published in 1997. It was based on his father's poetic tribute to the neighborhood where he grew up.

Harlem, in New York City, has been the capital city of black culture in the United States for generations. It is also an important part of the family history of many African-Americans.

Myers used collage to illustrate his father's poem. He says that the technique, which involves cutting out images and pasting them

"Illustrating children's books is a trip. So many people are starving for images. Image famine in African-America. I think we are learning how important images are, how much they do."

IN HIS ART, MYERS LIKES TO MAKE COLLAGES USING AFRICAN-AMERICAN MAGAZINES SUCH AS *EBONY, ESSENCE,* AND *VIBE.*

together, has connections with African-American art forms such as jazz, blues, and quilting.

Myers has also written and illustrated picture books of his own. The best-known is *Wings*. It tells the story of a boy who is teased by the other kids at school because he can fly. Myers has also illustrated a collection of poems by African-Americans.

In addition to working on his books, Christopher A. Myers is an artist, a children's photographer, and a clothing designer. He lives in Brooklyn, New York.

≈

WHERE TO FIND OUT MORE ABOUT CHRISTOPHER A. MYERS

WEB SITES

SCHOLASTIC KIDS FUN ONLINE
http://www2.scholastic.com/teachers/authorsandbooks/authorstudies/ authorhome.jhtml?authorID=2369&collateralID=5249&displayName=Biography
To read an autobiographical sketch of Christopher A. Myers

———

THE MAIN CHARACTER IN *WINGS* IS IKARUS JACKSON.
THE NAME COMES FROM THE GREEK MYTH OF ICARUS, WHO BUILT
A PAIR OF WINGS AND ESCAPED FROM AN ISLAND PRISON.

Walter Dean Myers

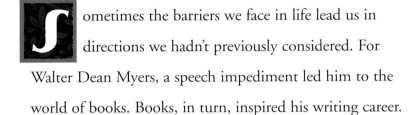

Born: August 12, 1937

ometimes the barriers we face in life lead us in directions we hadn't previously considered. For Walter Dean Myers, a speech impediment led him to the world of books. Books, in turn, inspired his writing career.

Walter Dean Myers was born on August 12, 1937, in Martinsburg, West Virginia. When Walter was two, his mother died. His father was very poor and had several children. The Dean family in New York City, who were friends of Walter's mother, offered to take in young Walter. His father agreed to send Walter to live with them.

The Dean family lived in Harlem, the largest African-American neighborhood in the United States. Growing up there Harlem gave Walter a child's perspective of African-American culture. He played basketball and stickball until it was too dark to see. He listened to the many languages spoken in the neighborhood. He went to plays at nearby Columbia

---

FOR FUN, MYERS ENJOYS PLAYING THE FLUTE, DOING CROSSWORD
PUZZLES, AND CHASING HIS CAT, ASKIA, AROUND THE HOUSE.

University, to church services, to Bible school, and to story readings at the public library.

Once Walter learned to read, he read everything he could get his hands on—from comic books to magazines and newspapers. A teacher brought him a stack of books one day from her own personal library. They opened up a whole new world for Walter.

Walter was a good student and could read very well, but a speech difficulty made it hard for him to communicate. He often retreated into books to escape this hardship. A teacher suggested writing down his thoughts and ideas as a way to overcome the problem.

Soon Walter was writing poems and short stories. By high school, Walter had discovered what he called his "avenue of value"—his way of finding self-esteem through his writing.

Because his family could not afford college, Walter Dean Myers left high school at the age of sixteen and spent three years in the army. Then he held various jobs, including loading trucks and working at the post office, but he never stopped writing.

Myers wrote at night after work. He was soon writing magazine pieces and advertising copy. When he saw that the Council on Inter-

> *"Books took me, not so much to foreign lands and fanciful adventures, but to a place within myself that I have been exploring ever since."*

MYERS WAKES BETWEEN 4:30 AND 5:00 A.M. AND WALKS FIVE MILES WEARING A WEIGHTED VEST.

A Selected Bibliography of Myers's Work

Bad Boy: A Memoir (2001)

145th Street: Short Stories (2000)

At Her Majesty's Request: An African Princess in Victorian England (1999)

Monster (1999)

Harlem: A Poem (1997)

Slam! (1996)

Malcolm X: By Any Means Necessary (1993)

Somewhere in the Darkness (1992)

Now Is Your Time! The African-American Struggle for Freedom (1991)

Fallen Angels (1988)

Scorpions (1988)

Motown and Didi: A Love Story (1984)

The Young Landlords (1979)

Fast Sam, Cool Clyde, and Stuff (1975)

Where Does the Day Go? (1969)

Myers's Major Literary Awards

2000 *Boston Globe–Horn Book* Fiction Honor Book
  145th Street: Short Stories

2000 Coretta Scott King Author Honor Book
2000 Michael L. Printz Award
1999 *Boston Globe–Horn Book* Fiction Honor Book
  Monster

2000 Orbis Pictus Honor Book
  At Her Majesty's Request: An African Princess in Victorian England

1997 *Boston Globe–Horn Book* Fiction Honor Book
  Harlem: A Poem

1997 Coretta Scott King Author Award
  Slam!

1994 Coretta Scott King Author Honor Book
  Macolm X: By Any Means Necessary

1993 Coretta Scott King Author Honor Book
1993 Newbery Honor Book
1992 *Boston Globe–Horn Book* Fiction Honor Book
  Somewhere in the Darkness

1992 Carter G. Woodson Outstanding Merit Book
1992 Coretta Scott King Author Award
1992 Orbis Pictus Honor Book
  Now Is Your Time! The African-American Struggle for Freedom

1989 Coretta Scott King Author Award
  Fallen Angels

1989 Newbery Honor Book
  Scorpions

1985 Coretta Scott King Author Award
  Motown and Didi: A Love Story

1980 Coretta Scott King Author Award
  The Young Landlords

racial Books for Children was holding a contest for black writers of children's books, he created *Where Does the Day Go?* He won, and the story became his first published book.

When Myers showed an editor a short story he had written about teenagers, the editor asked for the rest of the book. *Fast Sam, Cool Clyde, and Stuff* became Myers's first young adult novel.

During his career, Myers has

written picture books, middle-grade books, science fiction, fantasy, nonfiction, and mystery-adventure stories. He has touched on many important issues, such as suicide, teen pregnancy, adoption, and parental neglect. He has also worked with his son, writer and illustrator Christopher A. Myers.

Myers talks about growing closer to his characters as he works on a book, so that his readers can grow close to them, as well. Many readers feel as though the characters in his books quickly become old friends.

"Writing for me has been many things. It was a way to overcome the hindrance of speech problems. . . . It was a way of establishing my humanity in a world that often ignores . . . those in less favored positions."

&

WHERE TO FIND OUT MORE ABOUT WALTER DEAN MYERS

BOOKS

Jones, Lynda. *Five Famous Writers.* New York: Scholastic, 2001.

Jordan, Denise. *Walter Dean Myers: Writer for Real Teens.* Springfield, N.J.: Enslow, 1999.

Myers, Walter Dean. *Bad Boy: A Memoir.* New York: HarperCollins, 2001.

WEB SITES

EDUCATIONAL PAPERBACK ASSOCIATION
http://www.edupaperback.org/authorbios/Myers_WalterDean.html
To read an autobiographical sketch of and a booklist for Walter Dean Myers

———

MYERS BEGINS EACH NEW BOOK WITH AN OUTLINE.
HE THEN CUTS OUT PICTURES OF ALL OF THE CHARACTERS
FOR A COLLAGE THAT HE PLACES ON THE WALL ABOVE HIS COMPUTER.

Phyllis Reynolds Naylor

Born: January 4, 1933

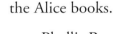

R eading and telling stories have always been an important part of Phyllis Reynolds Naylor's life. She has written more than 100 books for both adults and children, and she has won many awards for her children's books. Her best-known children's books include *Shiloh* and the Alice books.

Phyllis Reynolds Naylor was born on January 4, 1933, in Anderson, Indiana. Her father was a traveling salesman, so the family moved many times. During the summers, her family would go to either Iowa or Maryland to visit her grandparents. These experiences became a big part of the books that Naylor would later write.

Phyllis grew up during the Great Depression. Her family did not have much money, but

---

NAYLOR DOESN'T USE OUTLINES WHEN SHE WRITES. SHE FINDS THEM "LIMITING."

there were always good books to read. "My mother, and sometimes my father, read aloud to us every night," Naylor remembers. Her father even imitated characters while he read the stories. Storytelling is something she always remembers from her childhood.

As a young girl, Phyllis could hardly wait until she learned how to read and write. By the time she was in the fifth grade, writing was her favorite hobby. She would rush home from school each day to write a story. When Phyllis was sixteen years old, she had her first story published, in a church magazine.

After high school, Naylor went to college and studied to become a clinical psychologist.

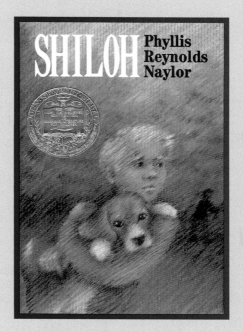

A Selected Bibliography of Naylor's Work

Bernie Magruder and the Bats in the Belfry (2003)
Blizzard's Wake (2002)
Alice Alone (2001)
The Boys Return (2001)
Carlotta's Kittens and the Club of Mysteries (2000)
Alice on the Outside (1999)
Achingly Alice (1998)
"I Can't Take You Anywhere!" (1997)
Alice in April (1993)
Shiloh (1991)
Bernie and the Bessledorf Ghost (1990)
The Witch's Eye (1990)
One of the Third-Grade Thonkers (1988)
Beetles, Lightly Toasted (1987)
The Year of the Gopher (1987)
The Keeper (1986)
How I Came to Be a Writer (1978)
Witch's Sister (1975)
To Make a Wee Moon (1969)
The Galloping Goat and Other Stories (1965)

Naylor's Major Literary Awards

1992 Newbery Medal
 Shiloh

"And so, because I want to know what it would be like to be a preacher or a bicycle courier or a motherless twelve-year-old or a bridge worker, I write."

As a student, she wrote stories and sold them to help pay for her college tuition. When she received her degree, Naylor decided that she wanted to be a writer. Since that time, she has been writing for both children and adults.

In her books for young people, Naylor is known for her ability to write from a young person's point of view. She writes both fiction and nonfiction books. Her books cover a wide range of topics. Her books have included advice on how to maintain friendships and ways to communicate with family members. Naylor's fiction books have explored many difficult issues that young people face today.

She has always written for both adults and young people. "I can never imagine myself writing only for children or only for adults," Naylor notes. "I like to follow up a mystery story for the nine-to-twelve set with a

"Whatever you have felt or seen or heard or done or even thought about doing—no matter how brave, how cowardly, how disgusting, or how adventurous—someone else has thought of too. When you put your thoughts and feelings down on paper, you can trust your readers to understand."

SOME OF NAYLOR'S HOBBIES ARE HIKING, BIKING, SINGING, AND GOING TO THE THEATER.

contemporary novel for adults. After that perhaps I will do a picture book or a realistic novel for teens, or possibly a humorous book for children."

Naylor lives in Bethesda, Maryland, with her husband and two cats. She continues write for both adults and children. Naylor says, "On my deathbed, I am sure, I will gasp, 'But I still have five more books to write!'"

❧

WHERE TO FIND OUT MORE ABOUT PHYLLIS REYNOLDS NAYLOR

BOOKS

Kovacs, Deborah, and James Preller. *Meet the Authors and Illustrators: 60 Creators of Favorite Children's Books Talk about Their Work.* Vol. 2. New York: Scholastic, 1993.

Hill, Christine M. *Ten Terrific Authors for Teens.* Berkeley Heights, N.J. 2000.

Naylor, Phyllis Reynolds. *How I Came to Be a Writer.* New York: Atheneum, 1978.

Nuwer, Hank. *To the Young Writer: Nine Writers Talk about Their Craft.* Danbury, Conn.: Franklin Watts, 2002.

WEB SITES

EDUCATIONAL PAPERBACK ASSOCIATION
http://www.edupaperback.org/authorbios/Naylor_PhyllisReynolds.html
To read an autobiographical sketch of and a booklist for Phyllis Reynolds Naylor

INTERNET PUBLIC LIBRARY
http://www.ipl.org/youth/AskAuthor/Naylor.html
To read an autobiographical sketch of and an interview with Phyllis Reynolds Naylor

―――――

SHILOH IS BASED ON THE TRUE STORY OF A STRAY DOG NAYLOR FOUND WHEN VISITING THE TOWN OF SHILOH, WEST VIRGINIA.

Joan Lowery Nixon

Born: February 3, 1927

Joan Lowery Nixon loved her high school English teacher. The teacher recognized Joan's talent for writing. She encouraged Joan to major in journalism in college. Nixon studied to be a journalist, but later she discovered her love for writing children's books. Joan Lowery Nixon has been writing children's books for almost forty years. Her best-known books include *The Kidnapping of Christina Lattimore, The Mysterious Red Tape Gang, The Dark and Deadly Pool,* and *The Other Side of Dark.*

Joan Lowery Nixon was born on February 3, 1927, in Los

NIXON GREW UP NEAR HOLLYWOOD, CALIFORNIA. SHE WOULD OFTEN SEE MOVIE STARS AND OTHER FAMOUS PEOPLE IN HER NEIGHBORHOOD.

Angeles, California. She lived in a large house with her parents and grandparents. Joan knew at an early age that she wanted to be a writer. She learned how to read when she was three years old and memorized words from her favorite books. She also asked her mother to write down poems for her.

In elementary school, Joan discovered her talent for story-telling. Her sisters and other kids from the neighborhood would gather in the family's playroom.

> *"Journalism taught me to focus because I had to sit down and write, whether I felt like it or not—no waiting for inspiration. I learned the skill of finding the important facts in a story, and how to isolate them from all of the unnecessary details."*

They would ask Joan to tell them a story or perform a play. With her mother's help, Joan wrote scripts for puppet shows. She also told stories using the dolls from her dollhouse.

Joan was always writing stories when she was a young girl. She even had a poem published in a children's magazine when she was ten years old. She became more interested in writing in junior high school, and she became the editor of the school newspaper.

After high school, she attended the University of Southern California. She met Hershell Nixon at the university. They married in 1949. After college, Nixon could not find a job in journalism. Instead,

NIXON'S HUSBAND, HERSHELL, IS A GEOLOGIST. SHE HAS WORKED WITH HIM TO WRITE SEVERAL NONFICTION BOOKS FOR CHILDREN ABOUT VOLCANOES, EARTHQUAKES, AND OTHER SCIENCE TOPICS.

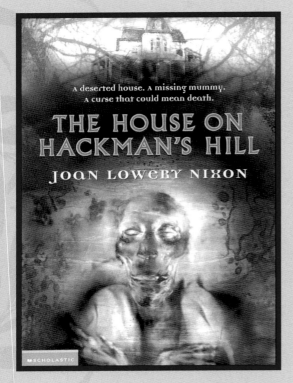

A Selected Bibliography of Nixon's Work

The Making of a Writer (2002)
The Trap (2002)
Gus and Gertie and the Lucky Charms (2001)
Ann's Story, 1747 (2000)
The Haunting (2000)
Aggie's Home (1998)
Circle of Love (1997)
Beware the Pirate Ghost (1996)
Land of Hope (1992)
The Weekend Was Murder! (1992)
Whispers from the Dead (1989)
The Dark and Deadly Pool (1987)
A Family Apart (1987)
Fat Chance, Claude (1987)
Haunted Island (1987)
Beats Me, Claude (1986)
The Other Side of Dark (1986)
The House on Hackman's Hill (1985)
The Stalker (1985)
The Séance (1980)
The Kidnapping of Christina Lattimore (1979)
The Mysterious Red Tape Gang (1974)
Mystery of Hurricane Castle (1964)

she took a teaching job in Los Angeles.

In the following years, Nixon and her husband moved several times throughout the country. By the time they moved to Texas, Nixon was the mother of four children. She was still interested in writing, but she did not have much time to do it.

While living in Texas, Nixon saw a notice for a writer's conference. She went to the conference and became excited about writing children's books. She worked for several years to write a book. When she finished the book, it was rejected by twelve publishers. Her first book, *Mystery of Hurricane Castle,* was finally published in 1964.

Since then, Nixon has written more than 110 books for children and young people. She has won many awards for her work, including three Edgar Allan Poe Awards.

Nixon continues to write mysteries as well as fiction and nonfiction books for children and young people. She lives with her family in Houston, Texas.

"I'm more challenged when I write for young people because when you write for 'children' you write for everyone from a two-year-old to a teenager. There are so many, many different styles and forms for these age groups."

WHERE TO FIND OUT MORE ABOUT JOAN LOWERY NIXON

BOOKS

Kovacs, Deborah, and James Preller. *Meet the Authors and Illustrators: 60 Creators of Favorite Children's Books Talk about Their Work.* Vol. 2. New York: Scholastic, 1993.

Nixon, Joan Lowery. *The Making of a Writer.*
New York: Delacorte Press, 2002.

WEB SITES

SCHOLASTIC AUTHORS ONLINE
*http://www2.scholastic.com/teachers/authorsandbooks/authorstudies/
authorhome.jhtml?authorID=68&collateralID=5252&displayName=Biography*
To read a biographical sketch of Joan Lowery Nixon, a booklist,
and the transcript of an interview with the author

AFTER HER FIRST BOOK WAS PUBLISHED, NIXON TAUGHT WRITING AT SCHOOLS, LIBRARIES, AND COLLEGES. SHE ALSO WROTE A HUMOR COLUMN FOR A DAILY NEWSPAPER IN HOUSTON, TEXAS.

Mary Norton

Born: December 10, 1903
Died: August 29, 1992

Everyone knows the Borrowers. Pod and Homily Clock and their daughter Arrietty may be only six inches tall, but they are giants in children's books. They became instantly popular when Mary Norton introduced them in *The Borrowers* in 1953. Four more books followed. Radio programs, television shows, and movies were made about the Clock family. Children everywhere loved learning about these tiny imaginary people, who lived by "borrowing" the small items "human beans" lost every day.

Mary Norton thought up the idea of the Borrowers when she was a child. She was born Mary Spenser on December 10, 1903, in London, England. She spent most of her childhood in the small country town of Leighton Buzzard.

On walks with her four brothers, Mary would lag behind, daydreaming. What would it

THE BORROWER BOOKS WERE INSPIRED BY NORTON'S POOR EYESIGHT. SHE CAREFULLY STUDIED THE SMALL THINGS SHE COULD BRING CLOSE TO HER FACE, GIVING HER THE IDEA OF A TINY FAMILY WHO ALSO NOTICED TINY THINGS.

be like to walk through this field of tangled grasses and thorn bushes if you were only six inches tall? How would you get through the gates that human children climb over so easily?

Mary imagined the Borrowers when she was very young. But she didn't write about them until much later. When she grew up, her first love was the theater. She became an actress at the Old Vic Theatre Company in

> *"In each generation, only youth is restless and brave enough to try to get out from under the floorboards."*
> —*from* **The Borrowers**

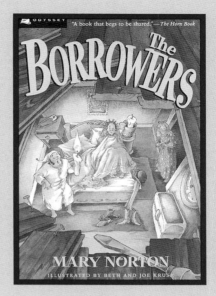

A Selected Bibliography of Norton's Work

The Borrowers Avenged (1982)
Are All the Giants Dead? (1975)
Poor Stainless: A New Story about the Borrowers (1971)
The Borrowers Aloft (1961)
The Borrowers Afloat (1959)
The Borrowers Afield (1955)
The Borrowers (1953)
Bed-Knob and Broomstick (1957)

Norton's Major Literary Awards

1952 Carnegie Medal
    The Borrowers

> *"I work terribly hard and sometimes rewrite a sentence six times over until the emphasis is on the right words and it falls in an interesting way. As long as one word sticks out like a sore thumb, I work on it until it reads so easily that nobody thinks I've worked so hard."*

London. Then she married Robert Norton and moved to his home in Portugal. Mary and Robert Norton had four children—Ann, Robert, Guy, and Caroline.

Mary Norton's life was turned upsidedown when World War II (1939–1945) broke out. She and the children moved to England, then to the United States, and then back to England. She did war work to help support the family. And then she began writing books.

Norton's first two books were about an apprentice witch, Miss Price, and the three children she makes friends with. *The Magic Bed-Knob; or, How to Become a Witch in Ten Easy Lessons* and *Bonfires and Broomsticks* later combined into one book called *Bed-Knob and Broomstick.* The books were very popular and were made into both a radio program and a Walt Disney movie.

When *The Borrowers* was published in 1953, though, Norton really became famous. Everyone loved the Borrowers—and reading about the dangers they faced from the humans who lived so close. Pod was brave, resourceful, and just a bit overprotective; Homily was loving but easily

NORTON ADORED BEING AN ACTRESS. SHE DESCRIBED HER YEARS AT THE OLD VIC THEATRE IN LONDON AS THE MOST MEMORABLE OF HER LIFE.

flustered; young Arrietty had a "questing spirit" that sometimes got her in trouble. You can learn a lot about life in England by reading the Borrower books. You can also learn a lot about what it means to be a human being—whether you are six inches tall or six feet tall.

Mary Norton died in her home in Devonshire, England, on August 29, 1992. She was eighty-eight.

✍

WHERE TO FIND OUT MORE ABOUT MARY NORTON

BOOKS

McElmeel, Sharron L. *100 Most Popular Children's Authors: Biographical Sketches and Bibliographies.* Englewood, Colo.: Libraries Unlimited, 1999.

WEB SITES

EASY FUN SCHOOL—THE BORROWERS
http://easyfunschool.com/article2083.html
For a literature unit on *The Borrowers* with suggested questions and activities

THE SF SITE FEATURED REVIEW: THE BORROWERS
http://www.sfsite.com/09b.bor41.htm
For reviews of Mary Norton's books and information about the author

———

NORTON PROBABLY DREW ON PERSONAL EXPERIENCE WHEN SHE WROTE *THE MAGIC BED-KNOB,* IN WHICH THREE CHILDREN LEAVE LONDON FOR THE COUNTRY DURING WORLD WAR II. SHE AND HER CHILDREN MOVED OFTEN TO ESCAPE THE BOMBING.

Laura Joffe Numeroff

Born: July 14, 1953

As a child, Laura Joffe Numeroff loved to draw, read, and make up stories. As an adult, the popular children's author still loves to draw, read, and make up stories! Although she has written close to thirty books, *If You Give a Mouse a Cookie* continues to be one of her readers' favorites.

Laura Joffe Numeroff was born on July 14, 1953, in Brooklyn, New York. Her father was an artist, and her mother was a teacher. "They both enriched my life with the love of reading, playing the piano, singing, dancing, science, and stamp collecting." Laura was the youngest of three girls. She has two older sisters, Emily and Alice.

NUMEROFF OFTEN VISITS LIBRARIES AND BOOKSTORES. SHE ALSO COLLECTS CHILDREN'S BOOKS.

Laura's favorite childhood possessions were her microscope, a box of sixty-four crayons, and her library card. She loved to read. She would check out as many books at one time as the library would let her have. She also loved to draw. Soon she was making up her own stories and drawing the pictures to go with them. She knew she wanted to be a writer.

"The best reviews come from kids who write me— that makes it all worth it!"

In high school, Laura decided to be a fashion designer like her older sister Emily. She went to the Pratt Institute in New York City to study fashion design. Unfortunately, she discovered that she didn't like fashion design!

While she was in college, Numeroff took a course in writing and illustrating books for children. During the course, she wrote a story for one of her assignments. The story was called *Amy for Short*. This became Numeroff's first published book. Numeroff forgot all about fashion design. She was going to write and illustrate children's books.

"I can draw no distinction between the words 'work' and 'spare time.' I love what I'm doing and the only time it becomes work is when there's rewriting."

Numeroff writes about everyday things and ordinary kids. Some of

NUMEROFF HAS HAD JOBS RUNNING A MERRY-GO-ROUND
AND WORKING AS A PRIVATE INVESTIGATOR.

IF YOU GIVE A MOOSE A MUFFIN

by Laura Joffe Numeroff
illustrated by Felicia Bond

A Selected Bibliography of Numeroff's Work

If You Take a Mouse to School (2000)
The Best Mouse Cookie (1999)
If You Give a Pig a Pancake (1998)
Sometimes I Wonder if Poodles Like Noodles (1998)
What Daddies Do Best (1998)
What Mommies Do Best (1998)
The Chicken Sisters (1997)
Two for Stew (1996)
Why a Disguise? (1996)
Chimps Don't Wear Glasses (1995)
Dogs Don't Wear Sneakers (1993)
If You Give a Moose a Muffin (1991)
If You Give a Mouse a Cookie (1985)
Amy for Short (1976)

her stories are silly. That's one of the reasons children enjoy them.

When she writes, she's affected by her own reading taste. "I prefer biographies, nonfiction and stories dealing with 'real-life' dramas—(I) never did like fairy tales all that much. I guess that's why my children's stories tend to be based on things kids actually go through, like wearing braces, being too tall for your age, being a daydreamer, having to wear something your grandmother gave you even though you think it's hideous," says Numeroff.

As a child, Laura Joffe Numeroff dreamed of becoming a writer, and that dream has come true. "I'll always have a first love for children's books. I hope to be writing until my last days," says Numeroff.

❧

WHERE TO FIND OUT MORE ABOUT LAURA JOFFE NUMEROFF

BOOKS

Holtze, Sally Holmes, ed. *Seventh Book of Junior Authors & Illustrators.* New York: H. W. Wilson Company, 1996.

WEB SITES

HARPERCHILDRENS
http://www.harperchildrens.com/pigpancake/
To learn about the book *If You Give a Pig a Pancake*

HOUGHTON MIFFLIN
http://www.eduplace.com/kids/hmr/mtai/numeroff.html
To read more about Laura Joffe Numeroff

LAURA NUMEROFF'S WEB SITE
http://www.lauranumeroff.com/
To read a biography and other information about Laura Joffe Numeroff

———

NUMEROFF ENJOYED BEING A GIRL SCOUT, ESPECIALLY SELLING GIRL SCOUT COOKIES. THIN MINTS ARE STILL HER FAVORITE!

playing, and his excellent grades, Robert enjoyed his high school years.

Conly started college in 1935 at Williams College in western Massachusetts, but the stress of being away from home got to him, and he dropped out during his sophomore year. After studying music and taking a few courses in New York City, Conly returned to college and got his bachelor's degree in English from the University of Rochester in Upstate New York.

After graduation, Conly took a job at an advertising agency and then went to work for *Newsweek* magazine. This marked the beginning of his successful career as a writer and editor. He married Sally McCaslin in 1943, and the couple moved to Washington, D.C. In

> *"Since I am in the writing business, when I get a story idea I write it down before I forget it. It isn't always for children, but those are the stories I most like to write."*

that city, Conly worked for several newspapers before landing a job at *National Geographic* magazine, where he worked for the rest of his life.

Eventually, Conly and his family moved out of the city. They bought a farm within commuting distance of Washington. When eye problems forced Conly to move back to the city, he used the extra time to pursue his lifelong dream of writing fiction.

In 1968, Conly's first novel for children, *The Silver Crown,* was published under the pen name Robert C. O'Brien. That title was followed

---

O'BRIEN LIVED ON A FARM. HIS FAVORITE PET WAS A SPARROW NAMED JENNY.

in 1971 by his award-winning *Mrs. Frisby and the Rats of NIMH.* In 1972, he published a thriller for adults called *A Report from Group 17.*

Robert Leslie Conly, known to the world as Robert C. O'Brien, died on March 5, 1973, of a heart attack. He was only fifty-five. His final novel, *Z for Zachariah,* was completed by his daughter and his wife, and published after his death.

> *"Children like a straightforward, honest plot with a beginning, a middle, and an end: a problem, an attempt to solve it, and at the end a success or a failure."*

"[His readers] write him many letters—smudged, misspelled, tremendously moving documents," Conly's wife once said. "A surprising number begin, 'Dear Mr. O'Brien, I too am writing a book.' These letters he considers extra sacred. They are . . . from the special children, from the dreamers . . . from our future writers."

❧

WHERE TO FIND OUT MORE ABOUT ROBERT C. O'BRIEN

BOOKS

De Montreville, Doris, and Elizabeth D. Crawford, eds. *Fourth Book of Junior Authors & Illustrators.* New York: H. W. Wilson Company, 1978.

WEB SITES

EDUCATIONAL PAPERBACK ASSOCIATION
http://www.edupaperback.org/pastbios/Obrienr.html
To learn about Robert C. O'Brien's life and work

———

O'BRIEN CHOSE TO WRITE HIS NOVELS UNDER A PEN NAME. IT WASN'T UNTIL HIS DEATH THAT HE WAS REVEALED AS ROBERT LESLIE CONLY, AN EDITOR AT *NATIONAL GEOGRAPHIC* MAGAZINE.

Scott O'Dell

Born: May 23, 1898
Died: October 15, 1989

S cott O'Dell had many different jobs before becoming a children's book author. He was a journalist, a cameraperson for movie studios, and a book editor. He also wrote many fiction and nonfiction books for adults. Later, O'Dell became an award-winning children's author. His best-known children's books include *Island of the Blue Dolphins, The King's Fifth, The Black Pearl,* and *Sing Down the Moon.*

Scott O'Dell was born on May 23, 1898, in Los Angeles, California. Scott and his family moved several times throughout southern California when he was a boy. He spent time exploring caves near the ocean and searching for fish and animals. He

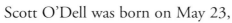

TWO OF O'DELL'S CHILDREN'S BOOKS, *ISLAND OF THE BLUE DOLPHINS* AND *THE BLACK PEARL,* WERE ADAPTED INTO FILMS.

grew to love the outdoors. This love for nature and the outdoors was often a theme in his children's books.

After graduating from high school, O'Dell attended four colleges. He never graduated from college. He only took classes that interested him and helped him with his writing.

When he left college, O'Dell joined a movie production crew. He worked as a camera operator on the filming of a movie in Italy. O'Dell wrote his first novel for adults while he was working on the movie. He also had several other jobs in the movie industry before becoming a full-time writer in 1934.

When O'Dell returned to the United States, he worked as a journalist, a columnist, and an editor. He also served as the book editor for a Los Angeles newspaper. During this time, he also wrote several fiction and nonfiction books for adults. O'Dell wrote adult books for twenty-six years before publishing his first children's book in 1960.

> *"History has a very valid connection with what we are now. Many of my books are set in the past but the problems of isolation, moral decisions, greed, and the need for love and affection are problems of today as well."*

Island of the Blue Dolphins was O'Dell's first book for young people. He got the idea for the story while doing research for another book. He

---

BEFORE BECOMING A WRITER, O'DELL WORKED ON A FARM.

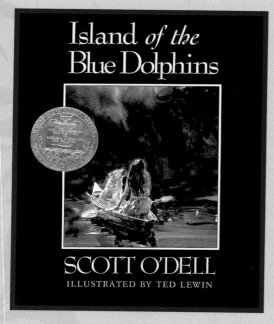

A Selected Bibliography of O'Dell's Work

My Name Is Not Angelica (1989)

Black Star, Bright Dawn (1988)

The Serpent Never Sleeps: A Novel of Jamestown and Pocahontas (1987)

Streams to the River, River to the Sea: A Novel of Sacagawea (1986)

Zia (1976)

The Hawk That Dare Not Hunt by Day (1975)

Child of Fire (1974)

Sing Down the Moon (1970)

The Black Pearl (1967)

The King's Fifth (1966)

Island of the Blue Dolphins (1960)

O'Dell's Major Literary Awards

1987 Scott O'Dell Award
  Streams to the River, River to the Sea: A Novel of Sacagawea

1972 Hans Christian Andersen Medal for Authors

1971 Newbery Honor Book
  Sing Down the Moon

1968 Newbery Honor Book
  The Black Pearl

1967 Newbery Honor Book
  The King's Fifth

1961 Newbery Medal
  Island of the Blue Dolphins

found a newspaper article about a young girl who spent eighteen years on an island off the California coast. O'Dell was interested in this story and decided to write a book based on this young girl. When it was published, *Island of the Blue Dolphins* received many awards, including the Newberry Medal. The book continues to be popular among young readers.

Most of O'Dell's books for children are historical fiction. He used this format to help

> *"I do want to teach through books. Not heavy-handedly, but to provide a moral backdrop for readers to make their own decisions."*

convey important messages to his readers. O'Dell used the themes of racial conflict, greed, and dealing with enemies in all of his books. Characters in his books also show great appreciation for animals, oceans, and the environment.

Scott O'Dell died on October 15, 1989, in Mount Kisco, New York. His last book for young people, *My Name Is Not Angelica,* was published the year of his death.

❧

WHERE TO FIND OUT MORE ABOUT SCOTT O'DELL

BOOKS

Kovacs, Deborah, and James Preller. *Meet the Authors and Illustrators: 60 Creators of Favorite Children's Books Talk about Their Work.* Vol. 1. New York: Scholastic, 1991.

McElmeel, Sharron L. *The 100 Most Popular Children's Authors: Biographical Sketches and Bibliographies.* Englewood, Colo.: Libraries Unlimited, 1999.

Russell, David L. *Scott O'Dell.* New York: Twayne Publishers, 1999.

WEB SITES

EDUCATIONAL PAPERBACK ASSOCIATION
http://www.edupaperback.org/authorbios/ODell_Scott.html
To learn more about Scott O'Dell's life and work

SCOTT O'DELL WEB PAGE
http://www.scottodell.com
For answers to frequently asked questions about O'Dell
and information about the Scott O'Dell Award

IN 1982, O'DELL ESTABLISHED A BOOK AWARD FOR AUTHORS OF HISTORICAL FICTION FOR YOUNG PEOPLE. IT IS CALLED THE SCOTT O'DELL AWARD.

Mary Pope Osborne

Born: May 20, 1949

Because her father was in the army, Mary Pope Osborne moved many times when she was growing up. She had lived in Austria and in many different states by the time she was fifteen years old. She loved the adventure of moving and living a new place. This thrill of adventure and travel is something she uses in her books. Osborne has been writing novels, picture books, and nonfiction books for children and young people for more than twenty years. She is best known for her Magic Tree House series of books.

Mary Pope Osborne was born on May 20, 1949, in Fort Sill, Oklahoma. She had a very close relationship with her parents, brothers, and sisters. This closeness made it easier when they moved to a new city. She loved to see new things when her family moved. She remembers a castle that was near their house in Austria and an old fort in Virginia. These and other

OSBORNE WAS ELECTED PRESIDENT OF THE AUTHOR'S GUILD IN 1993. THIS IS THE OLDEST ORGANIZATION OF PROFESSIONAL WRITERS IN THE UNITED STATES.

memories are part of the books she writes.

Her father retired from the army when Mary was a teenager, and the family moved to a small town in North Carolina. Mary missed the adventure of moving to different cities. She became involved in a community theater group where she found great adventure again. She worked both backstage and as an actor, performing many different roles in drama productions.

Osborne went on to study drama at the University of North Carolina. When she finished college, she traveled with a group of people throughout Asia. It was an exciting but dangerous trip. Osborne got very sick, spent two weeks in the

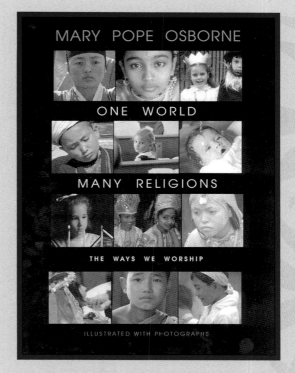

A Selected Bibliography of Osborne's Work

After the Rain (2002)
Good Morning, Gorillas (2002)
New York's Bravest (2002)
Space (2002)
Adaline Falling Star (2000)
Tigers at Twilight (1999)
Standing in the Light: The Captive Diary of Catherine Carey Logan, Delaware Valley, Pennsylvania, 1763 (1998)
Dolphins at Daybreak (1997)
Midnight on the Moon (1996)
One World, Many Religions: The Ways We Worship (1996)
Mermaid Tales from around the World (1993)
Spider Kane and the Mystery at Jumbo Nightcrawler's (1993)
Dinosaurs before Dark (1992)
Spider Kane and the Mystery under the May-Apple (1992)
American Tall Tales (1990)
Favorite Greek Myths (1989)
Run, Run As Fast As You Can (1982)

Osborne's Major Literary Awards

1997 Orbis Pictus Honor Book
One World, Many Religions: The Way We Worship

> *"Twenty years and forty books later, I feel I'm one of the most fortunate people on earth. I've journeyed through Greek mythology, Norse mythology, medieval stories, and American tall tales. I've 'met' George Washington and Ben Franklin, and without leaving home, I've traveled around the globe, learning about world religions."*

hospital, and had to return to the United States.

Back home, Osborne went to work as a travel consultant in Washington, D.C. One night she went to see a play. As she watched the play, she fell in love with one of the actors, Will Osborne. They met, and she married him about one year later.

After her marriage, Mary Pope Osborne traveled with her husband. He was in plays and productions across the United States. One day she decided to try writing a book. When she completed the story, she showed it to an editor who was very pleased with it. Osborne's first book for young people, *Run, Run As Fast As You Can,* was published in 1982. She went on to write many other books for children and young people.

Osborne has written more than twenty-five books in the Magic Tree House series. The stories are about two kids who discover a tree house full of books. Each one of the books lets them magically go to different times

―――

WHEN OSBORNE BECAME ILL DURING HER TRIP THROUGH ASIA, SHE READ ALL THREE BOOKS OF J. R. R. TOLKIEN'S LORD OF THE RINGS TRILOGY.

and places. In her books, Osborne helps her readers learn about history, people, and places throughout the world.

Osborne continues to write books for children and young people. She lives with her husband in New York and in their cabin in Pennsylvania.

> *"The wonderful thing about a career as a children's book writer is that there are so many different forms in which to fill different sorts of content. Choosing the vehicle that will carry a new story or passion into the world is half the fun."*

WHERE TO FIND OUT MORE ABOUT MARY POPE OSBORNE

BOOKS

Rockman, Connie C., ed. *Eighth Book of Junior Authors and Illustrators.* New York: H. W. Wilson Company, 2000.

WEB SITES

EDUCATIONAL PAPERBACK ASSOCIATION
http://www.edupaperback.org/authorbios/Osborne_MaryPope.html
To read a biography of Mary Pope Osborne

KIDSREAD.COM
http://www.kidsreads.com/authors/au-osborne-mary-pope.asp
To read an interview with Osborne and other information about her life

THE MAGIC TREE HOUSE
http://www.randomhouse.com/kids/magictreehouse/home.html
To learn more about the Magic Tree House series

OSBORNE RECEIVES MORE THAN **500** LETTERS EACH MONTH FROM MEMBERS OF THE MAGIC TREE HOUSE FAN CLUB.

Helen Oxenbury

Born: June 2, 1938

Helen Oxenbury knows that being a baby can be hard work. She watched her own three children struggle with learning to dress themselves, share toys, and make friends. Working at home as a children's book illustrator, Oxenbury began to wonder why there were no books made just for babies. Finally, Helen Oxenbury sat down at her drawing table and created her own version of a perfect baby book. Almost as soon as Oxenbury's first titles were published, they began flying out of bookstores and into the hands (and mouths) of grateful babies.

———

OXENBURY GREW UP IN ENGLAND DURING WORLD WAR II
AND REMEMBERS DRINKING TEA WITH HER FAMILY IN THE GARDEN AT
NIGHT AFTER AIR-RAID SIRENS REQUIRED THEM TO EVACUATE THE HOUSE.

Helen Oxenbury was born on June 2, 1938, in Suffolk, England, just before the start of the World War II (1939–1945). Suffolk, she says, inspired her to become an artist. Sometimes the sky was clear, and other times it was gray and gloomy, but it always made an impression on her.

Her parents encouraged Helen's early love of drawing. Her father, an architect, picked out her best pictures, and entered them in drawing contests. Helen usually won—exactly as her father expected. When she told her parents that, instead of going to college, she planned to attend art school in London, they happily agreed with her plan.

In London, she became close friends with a fellow art student studying illustration named John Burningham. Oxenbury longed for a career in theater design. When she finished school, she took a job with a small theater company. She loved creating bold, bright designs that gave audiences a sense of being in a different world.

> *"I can't remember any bedtime stories my father made up. I think these were potentially very good, but he had the maddening habit of dropping off to sleep before the end."*

Oxenbury and Burningham married in 1964. They had their first child a few years later. As a new mother, Oxenbury found her long hours at the theater difficult. Burningham, who was a well-known children's book illustrator, encouraged Oxenbury to try creating her own books.

OXENBURY GREW UP A GREAT FAN OF THE BABAR
BOOKS BY JEAN AND LAURENT DE BRUNHOFF.

A Selected Bibliography of Oxenbury's Work

Alice's Adventures in Wonderland (Illustrations only, 1999)
It's My Birthday (1994)
The Three Little Wolves and the Big Bad Pig (Illustrations only, 1993)
We're Going on a Bear Hunt (Illustrations only, 1989)
Pippo Gets Lost (1988)
All Fall Down (1987)
Clap Hands (1987)
Say Goodnight (1987)
Tickle, Tickle (1987)
I Hear (1986)
I Touch (1986)
Playing (1981)
The Dragon of an Ordinary Family (Illustrations only, 1969)
The Quangle Wangle's Hat (Illustrations only, 1969)
Numbers of Things (1968)

Oxenbury's Major Literary Awards

1999 Kate Greenaway Medal
  Alice's Adventures in Wonderland

1969 Kate Greenaway Medal
  The Dragon of an Ordinary Family
  The Quangle Wangle's Hat

So Oxenbury started working as a children's book illustrator. In time, she began work on her first book especially for babies. Babies, she knew, need books small enough to fit in their tiny hands yet sturdy enough to withstand chewing. Babies also like simple drawings in clear, bright colors. She showed her book to friends in the publishing business. They agreed that board books for babies were a great idea whose time had come.

In 1969, Oxenbury won her first Kate Greenaway Medal for her illustrations of *The Quangle Wangle's Hat* by Edward Lear and *The Dragon of an Ordinary Family* by Margaret Mahy. Oxenbury's other well-known titles include *We're Going on a Bear Hunt, Say Goodnight, Clap Hands,* and many books featuring the characters Tom and Pippo. Tom is a young boy, and Pippo, a stuffed monkey, is Tom's constant companion and very loyal friend.

> *"When I actually began to illustrate, with* Numbers of Things, *I found it enormously satisfying, and seven books . . . four years, and two children later, I still find it so."*

In the late 1990s, Oxenbury created illustrations for a new version of Lewis Carroll's *Alice's Adventures in Wonderland.* Using a combination of watercolor and black-and-white line drawings, she made Alice a confident, fearless modern girl. She was truly surprised when, in 1999, she was again awarded the Kate Greenaway Medal.

❧

WHERE TO FIND OUT MORE ABOUT HELEN OXENBURY

BOOKS

De Montreville, Davis, and Donna Hill, eds. *Third Book of Junior Authors.* New York: H.W. Wilson Company, 1972.

McElmeel, Sharron L. *100 Most Popular Picture Book Authors and Illustrators: Biographical Sketches and Bibliographies.* Englewood, Colo.: Libraries Unlimited, 2000.

WEB SITES

HALL KIDS ILLUSTRATORS
http://hallkidsillustrators.com/O/9.shtml
To find a list of Helen Oxenbury's titles with links to summaries and reviews

———

OXENBURY HATED SCHOOL, BUT SHE ENJOYED TENNIS AND PLAYED IT ALMOST CONSTANTLY BEFORE TAKING ART CLASSES AT IPSWICH SCHOOL OF ART.

INDEX